WHAT is the FATHER LIKE?

WHAT is the FATHER LIKE?

A Devotional Look at How God Cares for His Children

W. PHILLIP KELLER

BETHANY HOUSE PUBLISHERS
Minneapolis, Minnesota 55438

Published by Bethany House Publishers
A Ministry of Bethany Fellowship, Inc.
11300 Hampshire Avenue South
Minneapolis, Minnesota 55438

Printed in the United States of America.

Library of Congress Cataloging-in-Publication Data

Keller, W. Phillip (Weldon Phillip), 1920–
    What is the Father like? / W. Phillip Keller.
        p.   cm.
    ISBN 1–55661–722–4 (pbk.)
    1. God—Fatherhood. I. Title.
BT153.F3K45   1996
231'.1—dc20   96–4535
                                                          CIP

Other Books by
W. Phillip Keller

In Memory

of

my Dad,

who

truly, truly knew God!

W. PHILLIP KELLER, one of the premier devotional writers of our time, is the author of more than 40 books. Born in Kenya, the author studied in Canada to be an agrologist. He is also a photographer, field naturalist, conservationist, and lay minister. He lives in Canada with his wife, Ursula.

"Absolutely tender
Infinitely true
This is God our Father
Understanding you!

Absolutely lovely
Exquisitely near
This is God our Father
Nought have we to fear!"

Ancient Chorus

"This is life eternal,
that they might know thee
the only true God,
and Jesus Christ,
whom thou hast sent!"

—Christ Jesus

John 17:3

Contents

"I Am the Author"

I am the Author of all truth, all life. Before an event comes into being in your life I know it. I have authored it.

I am the eternal One, who has planned to disclose myself to you. When you seek me earnestly, when you yearn for my presence, when you long to know me as I am in reality—it is because I am calling to your soul.

Yes, I call for you, and I come to you, my beloved child, because I yearn to meet you. I await your love and childlike trust. And the more you get to know me the more you will trust me.

Open your heart to me now . . . just like a child. I am

your Father . . . and your Friend . . . your companion on all the pathways of your life. I am never far away. I am present with you, to preserve and enrich every moment of your life. For I hold in my hand all things that concern you. I have planned . . . I have authored . . . all the circumstances of your life.

All the circumstances that I authorize are intended to reveal—in the fabric of your life—that I arrange your circumstances in order to make clear to you the vast breadth of my character. I want you to know there is nothing that can happen to you that is out of my control. In everything I invite you to draw near to me. Be very sure I am near to you. And I understand you fully!

⁓

Though some aspects of your life make you view me as distant, a stranger, I am at work to help you know me personally as Lord of your whole life. When life tempts you to run—sit still! . . . and be open in my presence. You will be stirred . . . touched . . . and yes, transformed by our encounter.

My friend, I wait for you with open arms. I call you into my family. I rejoice at the prospect of sharing all my eternal life with you. Your life will be such a joyous adventure as you learn to walk with me. Knowing that I am the author of your life brings a brand new dimension into the commonness of your days. This, in actual fact, is how you begin to experience eternal life—as you open yourself and share in my supernatural life now.

I am . . . really . . . with you.

I ask you to remain open to me—calm and quiet—as I continue to reveal intimate insights into both my character and my actions toward you. As you know *me* better, you will better understand my *ways*. Knowing me will make it reasonable for you to trust my work in you completely. Knowing me will empower you to comply with my highest wish for you—which is to transform you in peace, joy, hope, and love.

I cherish you, my child. Be of great good cheer. Draw near to me now! Do not fear, for I have only the best intentions toward you.

As you quietly contemplate my full, loving authority you will begin to "see" with deeper spiritual perception that all of your life has both its beginning and its end in me. From the cradle to the grave, and beyond into eternity, I care for you . . . I hover over you . . . I teach you the childlike faith that causes you to rest in me.

Trust in me! I am the initiator . . . and I am the end of all things. What happens to you today has its origin in my enduring love. Every event is meant to increase your inward rest in my power . . . to open you up to the flow of my everlasting life in you. *I am* the author and finisher of your faith.

Be still . . . and I will create in your soul . . . serenity.

Read, reflect, and in faith respond to:

Hebrews 12:2; 13:8
John 8:58; 10:10; 17:3
Deuteronomy 7:9
Malachi 3:6
Jeremiah 29:11

1

"I Am the Word"

I am the Eternal One. I am your everlasting Father, and I do not hide myself from you or veil my plans in mystery. There are those who think I cannot be known. But the opposite is true.

From the first I am He who has come to commune with my children. I came to show my concern, to tell you in words of truth and simple terms what I am like.

Again and again I have spoken plainly, and even audibly to plain people. All that I articulate—in my Word, in your thoughts, or in wise counsel I direct to you—has one purpose: I want you to know me, and to know I am flawless. I am wholesome and utterly whole.

In a word, I am *holy*. When I declare my holiness, I do not mean to alarm you, or to distance you from me. Rather, my wholesome, whole, and holy character is my greatest honor, my greatest glory. Yes, my great glory is my perfect and complete nature.

This word that I have spoken to you is a verbal expression of my character—because it is a self-revelation of my very being, so you will know me and not fear me in the wrong way.

My nature, my conduct, and my desire to converse with you are easily seen in my words. There is no need for you to be in doubt about me, or to wonder about my amazing purposes for you. There is no need for you to be in turmoil about the good and simple design I have built into life itself—my pattern—for well-being.

I long for you to trust and rest in my Word. It is part of me, authored my me. It is shaped and arranged by me for your benefit. It is transmitted to you in truth. It conveys my Spirit and my life to you. Never shy away from my Word!

Instead, learn to immerse yourself, as in warm waters, in all the promises and statements spoken for your assurance. Though much of what men and women say is unreliable, though their words can be entangled with deception, doubt, and double-dealing . . . not so with me! My Word is absolutely trustworthy.

My Word is unbreakable, enduring forever because I am forever. It does not vacillate or change. For I am the same, never changing. I am always and ever the unchangeable One.

My child, all that lies beneath heaven is in upheaval and change. Nothing in creation lasts—

not the mountains

not the oceans

not the stars
not the sky or planet itself.
Every human relationship changes, every organization and civilization is in flux. Everything known to the human race ends, dissolves, and is no more.

Do you see why I have come to speak with you? Do you understand why I invite you to come to me, and know me through my Word, to learn to trust and love me dearly? For I offer you life in me . . . life eternal, in an eternal home I have created for you.

I am not like your friends and family, who can be fickle, unfair, and unfaithful. You can count on me. You can ground your entire life and your future on my goodness. Because of my unchanging good, I am God. You can be utterly at rest and repose in me because my commitments made to you are not broken . . . not altered.

Is it not the best news in all the world—to discover there is someone you can fully trust, whose Word you can believe?

Can you now comprehend why I say, "The words which I speak unto you, they are Spirit and they are life"? They convey the very essence of my gracious Spirit to you. If you take them in and believe them, they impart the very energy of my own eternal *life* to you.

Receive my Word. Taste my Word. Ruminate in my Word. Digest and assimilate my Word into your life by acting on it. In so doing you partake of me. You are participating in my life and share in my Spirit. You are in me, and I am in you.

As you learn to live in my Word, you will discover that it is vested with enormous potency, for I am the Most

High. My Word carries within it *might* and *majesty*. All that I command, all that I correct, I do in love.

What I am telling you will give you access to the place that is my peace. As you enter into a daily, living encounter with me, you will discover a dimension of love that is new every moment. Live in my enduring love.

Love me. And in loyalty to me, carry out my commands. Obey my instructions. You will be astonished to find how much your life becomes energized by my Spirit. I pour out life generously on the one who obeys me gladly.

Contrary to what others in the world may tell you, my commands are not in error. They are not burdensome. They are given for your great good. As you make my Word part of your life, you will find that we are walking together on the trail of time in close communion. Your will and mine become one in all we do together. As my will and ways fill you, we come to dwell together in peace.

⸺⸗⸻

So ... invest all your confidence in me, and you will be repaid with steadfast love. Slip your hand in mine, in faith, and find that you are guided by one with impeccable character. Trust in me, and find a safe place for your soul to be at rest.

Learn to become steady in your walk with me. You will be astonished at how I honor your loyal trust. I delight to do wonders for you. I can move mountains for you—mountains of *doubt, despair,* and *difficulty*. I can heal your diseases, relieve your distress, restore the ravaged years. I can bring

gladness to your soul
soaring hope to your spirit
sweet serenity within.

24

Five minutes of implicit compliance with my Word will teach you more about my presence, more about my power to preserve you than five years of mere religiosity. Try me, my beloved, try *me*. And see how faithful I am.

Do you want a great new adventure? Calmly, quietly do what I ask of you. And from within you will know the freedom of life that comes in following me. Set out to do my will—and in the instant you do so, I am there enabling you to achieve every task.

Because I formed you with my Word, I am He who works in you. I formed your body, your soul, your spirit. When you both *will* and *do* that which pleases me, it brings honor and life to you. As you live life close to me—shaping your life to my Word—my life, my energy, my presence and power enables you to triumph against trouble.

Remember that in the creative work that spun the universe into being—in preparing a world for you to live in—I did it all by my Word, spoken in faith. Listen: I said,

"Let there be light," and there was light.
"Let there be a firmament." And it was so.
"Let the waters be gathered together...."
"Let the earth bring forth grass...."

All that I declare is done—whether today or in the far distant future.

So I say, be bold to trust me! Do not hesitate or hold back. Believe that in me all things are possible. Trust and have confidence. There is nothing too difficult for me to do! But one thing *you* must do....

Today, decide that you will live free from fear. Believe that I am. Allow my life to be in you. Now that I have showed you my character, let me bring about beautiful changes in your character.

No other
philosophy
or religion
or thought system
in all the world has the capacity to change men and women in the very ground of their being. In tenderness and in truth I take the toughest outcasts and fashion them into the nobility of heaven. I transform the prostitute into a princess, the renegade into a royal son. I turn the phony pretender into a loyal, loving servant. I turned the timid soul into a fearless lion of the Faith.

For the ultimate proof that my living presence is among you is when my likeness is shown in your life.

I work all across the earth. I work in the most un-promising places—in the most unlikely people.

My light
and my love
destroy the darkness
of Man's despair and degeneracy.

To those formerly dead to me in spirit, I say,
"Come."
In
solitude
stillness
seclusion
come and meet with me.
Quiet your heart now and know me.

I am your Friend.
Your Companion.
Your Beloved.

Come into the serene stillness of my presence. Come and find peace. . . . My Word to you . . . is . . . "Live in me . . . and all is well."

Read, reflect, and in faith respond to:

John 1:1–3; 6:63
I John 1:1–3
I Samuel 2:2
Leviticus 11:44
Psalm 119
Joshua 1:1–9
Acts 5:32
Philippians 2:12

2

"I Am Almighty"

*A*lmighty.
The sound is so ominous. Does it frighten you to think I am *all mighty* and *all powerful?*

I am not distant or detached. Never haughty, rude, or disdaining. Quite the opposite!

My strength enables me to care for you tenderly. In my mighty keeping you are safe. You need not be alarmed. Always when I have come to my own I come in peace and goodwill—whispering, "Fear not. It is I, be not dismayed!"

Today, I say to you,

"I come in might to put things right."

Let's reason together....

—∞∞—

For centuries many have been confused by the words, "The fear of the Lord." Many held me in terror, deceived into thinking that in my might I am unapproachable.

Mystery and misunderstanding was woven around me. And multitudes would not even dare to mention my name. I showed myself mightier than all other gods and they took me to be more vicious and cruel than those false gods. And the fear that I would harm or shame them kept them away.

But now ... my child, you are drawn into the circle of my family. You know me as your Father. Now cherish me as your Friend.

I do not want you to live in craven fear and mistrust of me. I welcome you to meet me boldly. Today, despite any fear and misgivings, draw near!

I am mighty ... mighty in compassion to those who are contrite in spirit. Let me remind you it is the gentle who are strong. The mightiest are those who can lift up the fallen. The most powerful are those who can produce peace.

Come to me without your fear, and learn about my might....

—∞∞—

My might is beyond physical power. It transcends the energy of the cosmos—though all the dynamic flow of the universe has its source in me. And all the complex, meticulous laws of the physical universe were established and set in motion by my strength: Its order, precision, beauty, and progress are all evidence that I am at work everywhere, at all times. But my might is a force that brings wholeness, rightness, and justice of unfathomable depth. My might turns chaos and wrong . . . to *good*.

Yes, you can begin to know something of my might as you examine the uncanny order of your world, your cosmos. For my magnificent order is seen everywhere—in mathematics, physics, chemistry, biology. All will show you my design. Only the arrogant scoff at my supremacy in all things.

It is pride that blinds, self-centeredness that alienates them. Their false superiority is their downfall. Thinking they are wise, they demonstrate their folly.

And so, as the "wise" of the world argue and resist— let me show you the true measure of my might. For my might is contained in meekness. My enormous strength is poured out only to benefit others. From me there flows a never-failing stream of life, and anyone who drinks of it finds only *good*.

My might-in-meekness, my strength-in-giving, my streaming goodness—all were poured out for you in one life. The life of my Son. Stare long and hard into my mysterious might and you will know more about me than if you understand all the secrets of the universe. For I— God—came to you as a man.

I was born into a humble family, by a gentle virgin who was betrothed to a common carpenter. I saw no shame in this lowly lineage. The superb power of my Spirit overshadowed this young woman and caused her to conceive. A majestic demonstration of my might!

I was delivered in a crude shepherd's stable. My birth was attended by livestock, startled sheep-men, and ecstatic angels. Simple, yet supreme in all of history. I came in flesh to proclaim the glad news: "Immanuel—God is with you!"

My boyhood was spent in obscurity, in the nondescript, rough, crossroads town of Nazareth. A place notorious for the crude traders who passed through, bringing with them salt and silks, jewels and slaves. Sordid men making Nazareth a cesspool of corruption. It was here that I grew and matured.

At an early age I took my apprenticeship as a carpenter and tradesman, living and working amid the rub of common people. I saw

greed
squabbling and fighting
lying
abusiveness.

I labored among rascals
roustabouts
adulterers
religious men
hypocrites.

Yet because of the quiet power within me I was not corrupted.

Still a youth, I was given the noble honor of visiting the great temple in Jerusalem. I felt at ease amid those massive pillars. After all, it was my Father's house, erected to his honor. There I found enormous enthusiasm in deep discussions with the priests about eternal truth—my truth.

They had no clue who I was. They were baffled by my insights. So, too, were Joseph and Mary. But it was not a point of pride with me. No need to parade my wisdom. No need to assert myself.

Back in Nazareth, I worked diligently—with hammers, saws, and chisels—for many more years. I did not feel deprived by such heavy labor. I did not consider myself a victim of circumstances. I was not embarrassed by my crude environment or my humble home.

Amid the sawdust, the shavings, the planks of oak, wild acacia, and cedar I could live a true victor. As the carpenter of Nazareth, I was known for the quality of my yokes, beds, tables, and benches. I became known for fair prices, fair wages, and honest dealings. All of it was part of my power, my influence, and my impact on people.

Yes, yes, my friend, I know all about the way your everyday common people loved to drop into my simple shop—maybe to seek shelter from the sun, or to speak of some heartache, or to trade stories, with the smell of more than the tantalizing fresh-sawn cedar in our nostrils. And always they were drawn to my strength, my serenity.

The children especially were drawn to my dusty workshop. They ran their fingers through the shavings on my bench. They twiddled their toes in the sawdust on the floor. They wanted to hold and hug me. I in turn hugged them, long and tenderly. . . .

I tell you, my might is most wonderfully seen in day-to-day events. That is how ordinary people get a glimpse of the divine. That is why I say, "He that has seen me has seen the Father."

Once I laid down the carpenter tools and went out to live a more public life—somewhat like the prophets of old—there were more dramatic demonstrations of my might.

I turned water into wine, delicious and refreshing.
I healed the sick people by my word.
I stilled the gusting winds and high waves.

I broke the bonds of death and raised the dead.
I loved the lost and despised and saw their hearts.
I turned a few buns and fishes into
    banquets for thousands.
I set possessed people free from the
    tyranny of demons.
I explained truth in simple parables
    anyone could grasp.
I won the loyalty of tough people.
I went through all the anguish of
    a crucifixion for your sake.
I overcame death, corruption.
I rose from the tomb in a tremendous
    burst of resurrection power and life!

Yet, none of these demonstrations were meant to *parade* my power in pride. They were not done for sensational show, nor designed to impress people with my prestige.

No, all was done in service to you. For my greatest honor was the humble way I gave myself to God for your sake, whether I hoped to perform a miracle or to die for you. I hope you understand.

And so I tell you again, supreme strength is invested in me for your ultimate good. My might is intended for your care. My power is available
    to protect you
    to provide for you
    to create peace in your earthly pilgrimage.
Everything I am, and everything I do, is carried out in selfless service. That is the very root of my might. As I have told you by my Spirit, *I am Love*. No, I am not soft, sentimental, and sensual. But I am
    unselfish toward others
    self-giving to others
    self-sacrificing to benefit others.

In a word, I share myself with others to save them.

This secret of my might undergirds all the universe. The Enemy of your soul deceives you into believing that your highest purpose and pleasure in life is to please yourself, pander to yourself, and promote yourself. This dreadful deception destroys millions of souls.

But if you enter into me, my friend, you can call upon me, and share in my might. Gladly, freely, in great good will I bestow my life upon you. I pour out my spirit into your spirit, to saturate your soul, mind, will, and emotions with myself, and give you the power of Life!

In your human frailty—be filled with my power!

Read, reflect, and in faith respond to:

Genesis 17:1–2
Psalms 53:1–3; 91:1–16
I Corinthians 1:18–29
Luke 2:1–51
John 14:1–31
Matthew 20:25–28

3

"I Am Truth"

*I*n all the universe ... in all time and eternity ... in every decision you make ... nothing matters more than truth.

Do you understand what *truth* is?

In the simplest terms possible: What I say is absolutely true because I am the embodiment of truth, and all truth through all time has its source in me.

Truth stands constant and unchanging because it is grounded in my own constant, consistent character: I am wise as I am eternal. Truth that has its origin in me is the same. My truth remains the same from age to age, generation to generation, no matter how much men, cultures, or civilizations may change. So truth is a principle—if you will, a promise—expressed in a person's life.

The same . . . no matter what perspective you have; no matter how you view it; no matter from what angle you examine it. You cannot shift it around to suit your own purposes. My truth is

totally inviolable
utterly reliable
grounded in my absolute goodness.

But, my beloved, one aspect of truth escapes most people. . . .

———— ❧ ————

Truth remains only a theory unless you act on it in trust. Then it explodes with life from within, releasing a great force to set you free. Yes, *free* from

deception
falsehood
folly
bondage to sin
enslavement to your old self
and to Satan.

If you will act on truth, it empowers you to be free—free because you are following me. Your whole life is then loosed into the safety of truth . . . loosed into me. I am the Truth.

Unlike the best of human beings I do not disappoint you. I never deceive or double-cross those who trust me in their affairs.

I tell you this to save you endless heartache and trouble: The person who *lives* in truth—who perseveres in my instructions, who complies with my commands—will prosper in spirit. There is a discipline and high cost in keeping company with me. But your life will be an amazing adventure walking with me.

Pity the individual who spurns truth—who ignores it as unworkable, who rejects and ridicules my Word. He will be wrecked. By ignoring truth, your weary old world is breaking down under the burden of broken countries, broken homes, broken hopes, broken hearts.

Like the law of gravity, there is at work in the universe another law—the law of sin and death. It, too, pulls everything and everyone downward. It drags you down to do the wrong things in the wrong way, and has done so from the day you were born. Its force never relents. You can ignore it. You can scoff at it. And yet it will not stop exerting a formidable force and influence over you. So if you reject the strength I provide for overcoming the law of sin and death, you will be broken and pulled down by it.

Your society—your "wise" ones—scorn the very thought that there is a principle of sin-leading-to-death. That is why they reject
my Word
my truth.

They despise me, they scorn my people, they attack my messengers. And all the while they wonder what has gone wrong with the world. They lament that culture is in crisis. They fear violence and tragedy.

The world is a bedlam, poised on the edge of anarchy. People fear to trust each other. Promises are made to be broken. All of this because they have abandoned my truth and chosen to believe a lie—the lie that everyone can live as they like.

Catastrophe awaits them. . . .

But as for you, child ... *Live in truth.*

Act as one with me, and my strength, energy, and enthusiasm will lift you above the down-drag of sin and death. To obey me, to follow me in truth is to be set free ... to walk with me ... run with me! You will leap over every obstacle in life ... *with me.*

I have not hidden the truth from you. I have warned you—"In this world you will have trouble"—for the fallen world is endless trouble. But the rest of the truth is this: "Be of good cheer for I have overcome sin and death."

Come to me—daily, hourly, momentarily. And I come to you. I surround you and fill you with my presence. As we move together you are given the immeasurable resources needed to carry out my commands. As you live this way—centered in my truth—you share in my eternal Life. You find abundant life. You prevail over every evil that comes against you.

I am eager—keen and delighted!—to enter each aspect of your life as you open yourself to me and my Truth. I am able

to renew your mind
to calmly guide your emotions
to activate your will.

This is what it means to have me save your soul from slavery to your old self, to sin, and to your foe, Satan.

My presence with you and in you by My Spirit brings a magnificent purifying influence on all your life. My Spirit, my Word, and my power quicken your spirit. You become very much "alive" to me and to my role in your life. Because my Father and I are one in Spirit we now work in you to purge your conscience from all evil, making us all one in Spirit.

As spiritual truth dawns within you, you will begin to know my purposes for you. You will find yourself naturally communing with me in quiet confidence—your prayers will be prompted by my presence. You will discover profound satisfaction in sharing my life. This is how you pray in the power of the Spirit, in accordance with my will for you.

—∞∞∞—

Then . . .

Then you will be astonished to see me comply with your petitions. I will honor your intercession for others. Your prayers will stir good results in the world. My resurrection power will be made plain as I respond to your humble, earnest prayers. You will know, and see me at work within your spirit. You will see clearly how I am at work in the world.

My life and actions may be screened from the view of those dead to me, indifferent to me, in doubt about me. But you, my friend—you will march to another drumbeat. *You will be in step with my Spirit!*

All this is possible to the one who

lives

walks

and trusts

in my truth.

My truth will gain power over your mortal body. For I delight to take up residence with you, and in you. If you will allow me to care for you, soul and body, I can remake you completely. Your hot passions can be subdued by my presence. Your appetites can be contained by my power. Your selfish ambitions can be redirected into great benefit for others by my peace in you.

My child, I entreat you to give me the common ground

of your ordinary, daily life. Turn over the territory of your bodily behavior to my care.

What you drink
what you eat
what you wear
what work you engage in
what hours you rest
what exercise you get
what company you keep.

All your habits of health and hygiene are of interest to me. For I share your life and I reside in you.

I am Truth made flesh.

Do not be like those who say, "It's my body, I can do what I want with it!"

———

I am Truth, and I say,
I can restore your soul.
I can heal your diseases.
I can preserve you in peril.
I can make you to live in peace.

Turn over the control of your life to my care. And my truth will change you.

Read, reflect, and in faith respond to:

John 8:28–36; 14:1–14, 20–27; 16:29–33
Deuteronomy 10:12–14
Galatians 2:19–20; 3:1–2
Romans 8:1–28

4

"I Am Mercy"

*M*y friend, you live in a world that becomes more harsh, cruel, violent . . . and terrifying . . . with every passing day.

All over the world people pursue peace but find instead
turmoil
trouble
terror.

There is much discussion at the highest government levels aimed at bringing about humanitarian aid to hurting people. Yet civil conflicts, outrageous wars, cruel carnage, ruthless exploitation go on.

I am moved mightily by the abysmal cruelty and inhumanity of men. Just as I wept over the hardheartedness of Jerusalem, so I weep today over the cruelty on earth. Because I was crucified by iron-souled butchers, I am fully aware of the suffering and sorrow on earth.

No, I am not some unfeeling deity, as many people imagine me to be ... detached ... remote ... never feeling the pain of afflictions. I am not a casual observer. I walked among you. I bore your burdens. I was touched by all your distresses.

So now, I hear the groans of the injured with my *heart*. I know with my *being* the sorrow of those who lose their loved ones to violence and brutality. I grieve with my whole person over innocent people who are assaulted, abused, and maimed by human madness.

The cruelty of your cultures, the evil devices of your day, the wickedness of your world, still wound me. I am crucified in awful suffering by the sins of men and women who despise my mercy and who reject my grace, preferring to devour one another.

And because I suffered, I have won the authority to deal with you in generous grace and great goodwill, despite your awful attitudes and terrible atrocities.

Because I have suffered, I am all mercy. I am kind. I am grace, to help you overcome.

Mercy is my makeup, not a thin cosmetic application but in the essence of my character. It is my mercy that preserves the planet. It is my mercy that comes to you—amid all your despair—to bring you love, light, and my very life.

The plain reminder of my mercy is woven into my creation, so you will see it clearly every day....

Every morning you think, "It's sunrise!" The earth may be flooded with morning light—or the skies may be gloomy with mist, cloud, and rain.

Still, the absolute, ultimate truth is that the planet rotates in space on its axis, in a precise orbital path around the sun. So the surface of the globe is daily exposed to beneficent light and warmth as the earth spins and circles the sun. And its annual revolution guarantees a regular cycle of seasons—fresh growth in spring, the warm surge of summer, the plentiful harvests of fall, the quiet and rest of winter.

This continuous rotation and revolution of the earth is my doing—an order, created in my mercy, to perpetuate all life on the planet. All creatures—from a single-celled amoeba to the most intelligent human being—depends upon the sunrise to survive. If the earth stopped spinning in space, there would be utter destruction and death.

It is in my mercy
new every morning
shown in every sunrise
that good and evil people alike
receive of my kindness.

My mercy comes to all, spilling generously out of my *goodness* and my *care*.

So there is no special merit on your part that "earns" this mercy. So many malign me openly and refuse to let me govern their affairs. In arrogance they claim to be master of their own destinies (though every disaster they blame on me).

As it is with the sun that rises each morning, so it is with the rains that fall upon the earth. From season to season the vast storm systems move over the globe. They bring the rain, mist, and snow from the great ocean expanses ... to refresh the land ... to form lovely lakes ... to provide springs, streams, and rivers.

So few understand my care, my generosity—simple mercies—as they are given day to day. Many, in ignorance and folly, say, "There is no God!"

Yet in patience and long-suffering I never seek revenge, and though I am reviled I do not revile you in return. Though many spurn my grace, my goodness, my generosity, I continue in mercy—day to day—pouring out benefits on all the earth.

<hr />

With mercy like the rising sun ... mercy like the renewing seasons ... mercy like waters flowing ... to you. Hear my cry! For the end of an era is near!

My mercy flows, not only through the physical systems of the universe, but also in the moral and spiritual fiber of the cosmos. Were it not so, chaos and horror would rule. The world would be swallowed in howling darkness and slavery.

My mercy brings light, order, beauty, unity, and law into the spirits, the emotions, the will of men and women. It is my mercy that builds peace between myself and mankind ... between man and man.

All that is noble, uplifting, and inspiring has its origin in my mercy. Whether it is glorious music, lofty literature, fine art ... all find their fountainhead in my enduring goodness, my generous goodwill.

For in mercy I surrounded you with
rolling oceans
mirrored lakes
fresh-running rivers

streams and springs
bountiful fields
wind-rippled grasslands
deep-scented forests
budding flowers.

In mercy, the giant mountain ranges and the most minute organisms in the biota all came into being.

Yet . . . amid all this magnificent mercy, men choose to live in rebellion against me. They defy the laws I have established for their own well-being!

In puny pride, men prefer to cast off all restraints, indulge their passions, exalt themselves, exploit the earth, wreck their own environment, wage war upon one another, indulge violence and carnage.

Amid all this madness and mayhem the cry goes up from a million voices in anguish: "What's gone wrong with the world? Where is God? Why has He abandoned us?"

They cry because they have been deceived by a lie. The archenemy of their souls—my foe, the evil one—he whispers: *God has abandoned you. So go ahead and live in open rebellion and outright defiance.*

He whispers: *Go your own way. Live your own life. Make your own choices.* Instead of finding light, they fall in darkness. Instead of experiencing love, they find despair. Instead of discovering exuberant life, they are lost and dying.

My child.

My child! In mercy I come to you and to anyone who will receive me. I come to seek, rescue, deliver. . . . I come to set free those imprisoned by their own selfish interests and by their soul's enemy. To set them free of their enmity against me. . . .

53

No one can fully grasp the enmity that exists between the soul of rebellious man and his merciful Maker. The appalling pride of the human heart is set in a hard, defiant will against my gracious goodwill. In the darkness of their angry delusions men and women despise and reject me, though I do them great good.

I call you my children, and yet when I came to you humble as a child, Herod the king plotted my assassination. Later came the tempestuous three years in which I was under constant attack by the religious hierarchy. The priests and scribes could not "see"—or comprehend with clear spiritual perception—that I came to reconcile men to myself. Utterly oblivious to my divine nature, they charged me with being a devil—but in fact, it was they who made themselves enemies to me!

Various attempts were made on my life. In Nazareth, a crowd tried to push me off a cliff to my death.

Then had come the hour for my supreme sacrifice. In soul and body I gave myself to my foes to atone for *their* sin of anger against God.

So, a great mystery began to unfold . . . beginning with hours of anguish in the olive garden . . . the grim betrayal by my friend Judas . . . and the priests' midnight trial in a mock court . . . followed by the Romans' cruel whips, tearing thorns, and nails . . . the wooden cross against my broken body . . . my very lifeblood spilling out on the soil.

There I hung . . . mercy itself, extended to all men.

I could easily have saved myself. I chose to save you.

You see, my friend, genuine forgiveness extended to another costs a great price. The one who forgives literally lays down his or her life, in humble self-sacrifice, *to bear the cost of reconciliation*. It is a titanic transaction in which the merciful one takes on all the burden of the crime, the anger, the animosity—and sets his foe free. And that is what

I did on that awful hill of Calvary. All men and women of all time were set free because I took upon myself all your iniquities.

⟨⟩

Now you know why the peace made between you and me is so precious. Now you know why the reconciliation between sinner and Maker is sure.

All because, my child, I am mercy. And in grace I paid to wipe away your sins. No one else *could* pay that cost.

Because I am God.

Read, reflect, and in faith respond to:

Hebrews 4:14–16; 6:4–6
Matthew 23:37–39
Colossians 1:16–17
Exodus 34:6–9
James 1:16–21
Nehemiah 9:16–33
John 3:13–21
Luke 19:10

5

"I Am Understanding"

It sounds simple for me to say I am understanding. Not understanding in the worldly, sympathetic sense, but I am *all wise* . . . full of knowledge and insight into all that is best for you. Therefore, I care for you, in full and complete understanding of all that takes place in your life. So you can rest in me, in assurance that all is well because it is in my hands!

What a supreme solace for your soul.

What a supernatural strength for your spirit.

What a sure foundation for your faith in me.

But in your troubled world the remarkable fact that I understand all people . . . I know all about everyone . . . I am wise in all my ways . . . is quite alarming. I will tell you why. . . .

So many people hide behind a false front. From their earliest childhood they are taught to project a self-image of superficial success. They are given the notion that you can put on a fine appearance . . . as if they are using cosmetics to cover up blemishes.

But behind the facade their true character can be very corrupt. They become phony, pretending to be decent when they are not. This sort of cover-up is used for selfish purposes . . . to influence people to do things for you . . . to view you the way you want to be seen!

No wonder it's frightening to be told there is One who can see right through their cover-up. How terrifying to think the truth is known.

It is no surprise, then, that millions recoil from meeting me. Little wonder that

self-centered
self-assured
self-righteous

people seldom respond to my approach. Who wants to be found out, exposed, discovered?

Now you know why I say, "I do not come to call the self-righteous individuals, but rather those who recognize they are sinners, willing to repent of their wicked way." Now you can understand the indifference of some when you speak to them about me. They are not much impressed by your enthusiasm to introduce me. They would prefer *not* to meet me! The encounter would be unsettling . . . uncomfortable.

——⌘——

There is another reason most men and women are

alarmed at the thought that I am complete understanding. If it's true, it means they might have to submit to my direction. For someone who is all-wise and all-knowing does have the authority to direct their decisions. But that would mean giving up control to me!

The most formidable fortress of the human soul is the will—the inner insistence to demand its own rights. You contend that you have the absolute control of your own choices in life. You are determined to do your own thing, go your own way, be your own person—even if such independent decisions lead you to despair and self-destructiveness.

This iron-willed resistance to relaxing control over your life . . . trusting in my benevolent care . . . lingers long even in my children. So few fully relax in me, resting in my love and loyalty. It is an ongoing grief to me. . . .

Then there are those who will not submit their intellect to me.

I am not speaking of everyone who possesses the gift of intelligence. Do you suppose I value willful, lazy ignorance? No, I am speaking of those who have chosen to make their well-honed reasoning abilities a barrier against me.

Many of these men and women deeply resent me. They often reject my understanding of the universe. They heap ridicule upon my person and my wisdom. Some rant and rave openly against my knowledge, dismissing it all as irrelevant to modern man.

These haughty souls work hard to shape public opinion to deny my very existence. In their folly they reject my Word, my truth, my infinite wisdom—which I offer for their own benefit! In their ignorance and animosity they abuse my name and persecute the humble people who have put their explicit trust in me.

It has always been this way with cynics.

Let me remind you once again, my child, that—always, always—men and women must make a choice. Will they respond to my compassionate wisdom, or pursue their own path of prideful independence?

———

Still, I come because I am understanding. I understand that you will not seek me or find me unless I come to you first!

I look over your world and see parents who do not understand their youngsters. Children who do not comprehend their parents or other adults. Brothers set against sisters; sisters locked in vicious rivalries and misunderstandings. Men and women—who have lived together for twenty years—and yet do not understand each other! I hear every soul's anguished cry: "Oh, if someone just understood me fully!"

I know you yearn to be known. You long to be treated in fairness, mercy, and sympathetic understanding. And I am close to you now to answer that cry! I come near to every struggling soul who aches to be understood ... to be *known!*

To the ones who call out to me in frustration and need, I come. To the ones who are lost and dying inside ... dying of loneliness and isolation ... I come. It is never my will that any should perish. And then begins the great task—unfolding throughout your lifetime—of discovering just how much I understand all that pertains to you.

My understanding of you began ... long before you were born. . . .

—⟨∞⟩—

I and only I, the eternal living God, fully comprehend the complex arrangement of genes of your chromosomes.

From the instant of your conception in your mother's womb I am aware of all the characteristics and individual traits you inherited from your forebears. I understand precisely the way in which your parents, grandparents, and all those in your far distant past have contributed to your unique person.

Who else can claim such knowledge?

People are puzzled by one another's behavior. Baffled by unusual conduct. They criticize traits they cannot comprehend. Most people do not even begin to understand themselves!

Is it any wonder there is confusion and stress in human society? Misunderstanding heaped upon misunderstanding brings hostility, hatred, and cruelty. The world tears apart. Families fractured. Friends alienated. Isolated people sink down in despair. They turn to

lawyers

psychologists

counselors

psychiatrists

to try to sort out their troubles.

And all the while I wait patiently for you to turn to me for counsel, for wisdom, for rest. I am the supreme counselor.

Come to me, and first of all I will give you my peace. Allow me to lead you out of despair into delight. Follow me in quiet faith to find still waters in your soul as my love fills your life!

Because I know every fiber of your being I know you as no other can! I pity your weakness as a Father pities his children. I counsel you as your closest companion. I comfort you as your Friend. Just let me be all that you need in your wearisome world. Don't draw back—draw near!

———

I understand
every move you make
every place you choose to live, work, or play
every associate who molds your mind.

Astonishing as it may seem, in my infinite wisdom and understanding, I am acquainted with every thought, attitude, and choice you ever owned. You may be able to screen yourself from even your closest friend—but not from me! I know the worst and I know the best about you. Don't be alarmed! Instead, turn to me and know my concern for you.

I will never berate or belittle you. I extend my arms to you in welcome ... forgiveness ... in acceptance ... in warm goodwill ... just as you are ... this hour.

Come to me as you are today. Fling yourself completely into my care ... into my embrace....

You will be astonished at my understanding of you.

You will know peace and pardon because you have met me at last.

Read, reflect, and in faith respond to:

Psalms 34:1–22; 104:24–35; 139:1–18
Luke 12:22–32
John 1:47–49; 4:3–30; 15:14–17
Proverbs 1:33–2:7

6

"I Am Grace"

*W*hen someone meets me in a personal encounter, they are astonished to discover that I am grace. My whole person is pervaded by grace. I am powerful, yet approachable, because grace—my whole character of goodness—enfolds their life in great generosity.

Satan, the deceiver, who is your archenemy and mine, would have you believe I am harsh in judging your conduct, scrutinizing every little mistake.

But I am Grace.

Perhaps you do not understand this part of my character. My grace is not only my very nature—it is also the eternal goodness that governs all I do. Grace is the essence of my greatness, my generosity in dealing with the human race.

Perhaps you have sung the hymn, so loved by millions, that says,

"Amazing grace, greater than all my sins!"

Grace is a synonym for myself. *I am* greater than all your sins! I am the eternal God of all grace. I give and give and give myself to perishing people. My life is poured out to you—and that is my grace. The two cannot be separated one from the other:

My life, sustaining the cosmos, is my grace.
My life, redeeming the ruined, is my grace.
My life, making you whole, is my grace.

Many theologians engage in pontifical debates about grace—as though it were an excuse to create difficult doctrines.

My child, when you *come* as a child, you will have a firsthand encounter with grace. When you meet me as a child, you meet grace. When you fling yourself fully into my care, you are enfolded in my grace . . . myself.

All that I am
all that I do
all that I say to you
are expressions of my essential grace.

I came to your race in grace
    and goodwill at Bethlehem.
I lived among you, doing only good in grace.
I touched the fallen, the forlorn,
    with amazing grace.
I spoke forgiveness to sinners in instant,
    redeeming grace.

I laid down my life for all lost men
   in generous grace.
I vanquished sin, death, and the Enemy
   with great grace.
I rose in power and grace to be supreme
   Sovereign in the universe.
I am the God of all grace!

Consider the true story of one man who understood grace ... a gentleman of great honesty, humility, and honor. The man, Abraham Lincoln.

One day he passed by a slave auction where a beautiful black girl was on display. At the time, emancipation was not yet won.

When he looked into the lost, fearful eyes of this girl, he understood her terror. She would be misused by whoever bought her.

And the bidding began.

To the amazement of the crowd, Lincoln raised his hand to bid for this girl—prepared to pay any price for her. When at last no one would match his offer, the frightened girl was turned over to him.

In anguish she asked, "What do you want to do with me?"

Calmly, the great man replied, "I only want to set you free."

The girl could not believe him. No one paid that much, just to set someone free. "But you *are* free," he told her. "Free from your old burdens and the shame of slavery. I demand nothing of you. You are *free!*"

In that instant the girl knew what grace was.

"Sir," she replied, "I will go with you!" Set free, she

could follow her redeemer in gratitude.

It is exactly the same with me. I come to set you free—hoping you will follow me ... to be touched and transformed by my grace divine.

And yet ...

———

There lies a great misunderstanding about true freedom.

Men and women assume they have the inherent right to do just as they choose. They think it is freedom to indulge in the utmost folly, to engage in the most destructive practices. This is not freedom, but abject slavery of the worst sort. And so they become slaves to their own selfish passions, and by the power of sin and death that is at work in their desires. They are bound into submission by weakness of their flesh and of the devil.

And now evil is called good, and good is regarded as evil.

On television
in magazines
in films
in books
in music
goodness is despised.

My good is opposed by open wickedness. My gentle conduct is vilified by violence. My generosity is mocked by your selfish greed. My grace is brushed aside as a bad joke.

———

And still I pursue those enslaved. I search for them

down the tangled trails of their tears. I speak comfort to their sin-stained souls. I entreat them to turn to me in their rush to self-destruction in order to be set free from their past. Freely, I offer full forgiveness for all their wrongs.

No other gesture of goodwill comes close to my generous redemption of your soul.

That is just the beginning. . . .

Once you are mine you will *truly* know grace. All of my blessings
benefits
and bounties
are like rain poured out upon you freely. You do not work for them. You do not earn them. You do not pay a human price for them. They are . . . my gift to you!

In grace
I come to you
call you
choose you
accept you
cleanse you
console you
change you.

My child, come drink of my generosity . . . partake of my goodness . . . find overflowing benefits in my company.

As you give yourself—all that you are, all that you own—to me, I give myself to you. In this exchange you come to know me intimately. Firsthand you experience life given to you hour by hour. In simple, living reality it is I who comes to live in you, and you live in me.

I want you to partake of my eternal life now. It flows to you freely, graceful as a river . . . the River of Life . . . never ceasing!

This is my grace to you!

Read, reflect, and in faith respond to:

Numbers 6:22–27
Job 33:14–24
Isaiah 30:15–21
Luke 4:16–22
John 1:14–18; 8:32–36
Romans 3:20–25; 5:16–20
Ephesians 2:1–10

7

"I Am Long-Suffering"

*M*y friend, you live in a suffering world. A world
filled with sorrow.

That is because it is a realm ruled by the ruthless god
of your world—Satan, the despicable deceiver. He delights
in destruction. By using the law of sin and death, he drags
men and women down into degradation ... until people
misuse each other and believe it is normal.

Men have become hard. Women are calloused. They
say, "The world is hard." They've convinced themselves
that selfish behavior is in their best interest. Such a
world—where everyone preys on each other—is *abnormal.*
It is an outrage and an abhorrence to me. It goes against

all that is decent, noble, and right.

One day soon the cup of human iniquity will overflow with such pollution that it will demand a sudden end. There is coming a day of reckoning.

Meanwhile, I walk amid the anguish of my children. I suffer long with those abused and beaten. I am filled with remorse over your race, grieved over the transgressions of my people. I am here, suffering with you amid the flames of your afflictions.

It has always been this way.

From the very beginning of human history, my affection for you, my interest in your well-being, has constrained me to come to you constantly.

For countless centuries—across thousands of years of your horrendous human history—I have shared in your suffering. This is not empty rhetoric, not a pleasant platitude. It is sorrow upon sorrow, trouble upon trouble to me.

Because I am understanding, I knew before ever the earth was formed that evil would enter here. And I knew that I would come to suffer with you.

Are you astonished that I care enough to come to you? Are you startled to discover I am still here to help? So many think that I sit enthroned far above you, in the distant heavens, untouched by your pain. No, my beloved child, I am acquainted with all your anguish. I taste all your turmoil and trouble. I know the futility of your years in this vale of sorrows.

I am long-suffering. . . .

So often my greatest grief comes from my own followers . . . those who claim me as their Lord . . . their Father. Any human parent can grasp how deeply one's own children wound the heart. Those who are the closest cause the most profound pain. It is that way with me as well. The wrongs of my children wring my Spirit in sadness: their perverseness is a terrible pain: their transgressions are a torment.

Not only do your sins separate you from me, they alienate you from each other. I have pleaded with you to forgive each other. I have begged you to be big enough, generous enough, good enough, to go and extend peace and pardon to those who persecute you. It is the secret to serenity of soul.

All of my mercy, goodness, concern, grace, love, and generosity is poured out on you in a never-ending stream. Can you not, in turn, pour out the same sweet waters of blessing to others? If indeed you drink deeply of my supernatural life daily, there is bound to flow from you freely a stream of inspiration that can uplift those around you.

There does not need to be discord. My profound yearning for you is for peace and rest.

It is possible for us to be bound up in oneness, in harmony, in goodwill, as you take the forgiveness I have poured out to you and pour it out to others.

Sad to say, too often this is not the case. You let conflicts and confrontations disrupt our unity and tranquillity: You let your old self-life take over. It seems so easy for you to revert to your old ways, to return to your self-interests—to act as if I am not even around.

It is heart-wrenching to be ignored. It is such a sorrow to be forgotten and neglected by my children.

I know all about the pressures of daily life.

I am well acquainted with attacks and demands
of your world.
I am familiar with the expectations
of your family.
I am supremely sensitive
to your struggle to survive.
I know all the reasons
why you are so busy
and stressed.

Child, set aside time for me. It stirs my heart to know
you care enough to spend some of your day in serene solitude with me. These quiet, gentle moments together can
be very precious ... very rich ... for both of us.

In our quiet encounters you have a chance to unburden
your soul to me. And I, in turn, have the opportunity to
bestow my benefits on you ... to empower you to live with
my abundant life.

You do not need to come to me with stilted, formal
liturgy. You do not need to "praise" me until you have
whipped yourself up into an extravagant show of emotional excitement. That is not what I long for from you.
Oft-recited prayers and much shouting really do not impress me. What I yearn for is ... you.

I ache for you with an amazing intensity. You, your
race, your people were brought into being upon this planet
for one supreme purpose—that you might become my
dear children, conformed to my character, with whom I
can commune in harmony, for all eternity.

All that I am
all I have ever done
all my plans for you

are aimed at one sublime end...

that you should know me as I am. The surest way this will ever happen is for you to meet me ... again and again and again ... day after day ... best of all each morning, in stillness, solitude, and secret.

It takes time to know me. It calls for your attention, your interest, your willingness to wait for me to speak to you clearly. It requires you to come and find great delight in my company. It implies that you will begin to fulfill my wishes, obey my word to you, and trust me always to accomplish all I command.

This I long to have with you.

This is why I have been long-suffering from all eternity.

Unchanging ... is my patience as I deal with all those who seek to know me. I am not hard or harsh, but I pursue wicked people in compassion. I am not condemning, but I correct people to free them from the reward of their misconduct. I see beyond shortcomings—I see what you can become as you walk with me.

I tell you in truth ... my long-suffering prevails in drawing willful people into my family. Though it takes years and years, I never grow weary, nor do I give up. Wherever I see a struggling soul, I long to set that one free.

Suddenly it may dawn on you I have always pursued you down the tangled trails of your life. It did not matter if you dodged and darted, I pursued you, to seek and to save! In patience, I prevailed.

When you grasp my long-suffering, you can begin to take part in this aspect of my character. Your prayers of intercession for awkward, difficult people: your patience and fortitude in treating them in kindness. Your faith in me, to see beyond their shortcomings: your calm assurance I can reshape their sordid lives. Each of these gives the world a glimpse of my long-suffering in action. Together, we really do become co-workers, suffering servants, prepared to lay down our lives in eternal service to others.

Remember that when I was among you, my enduring effort was spent on the so-called "sinners"—the despised publicans, down-trodden prostitutes, and the demon-possessed. In their extremity, they responded to my call. They longed to be put right, and I did not disappoint them.

Today, the same miraculous work goes on. As I work patiently in you, I work in others. I work so that one day many more eyes will be opened, and many more humble hearts will declare, "God's hand has been upon me for good, all my days. Even when I was a stranger to Him, He drew me in patience and unrelenting love!"

Each of you precious people—who are brought into a new life within my family—make my long-suffering supremely worthwhile. You bring enormous satisfaction to me. You are mine, and I am yours . . . forever and forever.

Enter into my joyous, rewarding work of long-suffering. Know the pure joy of bringing the lost to me. I will sustain you, so you can put up with awkward people in patience.

Together, we can prevail!

Read, reflect, and in faith respond to:

Genesis 6:5–12
Isaiah 53:1–12
John 1:12
Psalms 46:1–11; 103:1–18
2 Peter 3:5–9
1 Timothy 1:14–17

8

"I Am the Savior"

*W*hen I entered your world, the angel heralded my coming, saying, "Fear not! I bring you good news of great joy, for all people everywhere. Unto you is born a Savior! He is Christ the Lord!" And for two thousand years, millions have sung this joyous message to the world over.

But so many are yet strangers to "the Savior." The majority have never met me.

One problem is that my birth has been wrapped in an aura of romance, poetic imagery, and fanciful imagination. My coming has been surrounded with the sweet sentiments of "the magical manger moment."

But for me, the moment of my entrance into your human society was the moment of my descent . . . the moment when I left the highest throne and entered a scene of supreme humiliation. I laid aside the majesty of eternal splendor to become your suffering servant . . . God, very God, in human guise.

In my coming as Savior, most men and women miss the titanic transaction that took place. I was not putting on a pantomime to impress you. I was deliberately entering totally into human life. I became as you are, so you can become as I am. I came to save you *fully*.

But the term "to save" is used to say so many things:
"I want to save some money."
"I want to save the finish on my furniture."
"I want to save that suit for a special day."
"I would be wise to save a soul."
What does it mean to save?

———

Savior . . . is my supreme title in all the universe.

From my perspective, this means I am He who delivers . . . sets free. I emancipate you fully from the dilemmas in which you live. I am the Savior, who alone can loose you from all the difficulties and distress of your human condition.

I can set you free from
deception in the world
snares of your Enemy
the guilt of past misdeeds
the grip of sin in your daily life
enslavement to your *self*
the regrets of wasted years.
I can set you free from an empty, hollow life, to live with

me in profound purpose and superb peace of soul.

The so-called wise ones of the world, and the devil himself—these will oppose all I tell you. But be of good courage! I come to you with clear guidance and wonderful wisdom established in my Word to you. I am the One who saves you daily from wrong decisions; from subtle deception spawned by the world system; from the delusion of your archenemy; from your own self-deception.

⸻⟡⸻

To save ... I have given you my Word. You will find absolute truth and sure solutions there.

Spend time meditating upon my clear instructions to you. Take them seriously. Act on them deliberately. Comply with my wishes for you. You will be amazed how, through my Word, I save you from your dilemmas and safeguard you from endless difficulties.

Let us take the matter of *success*—so important in your world! So many are convinced there is only one type of success. "Go for the *top*," they say. "Scramble for supremacy! Grasp for power and prestige and possession...."

These words prevail, but do not lead to peace, but to distress. Those at the top find they are hated and envied by their rivals who scheme to knock them down. They are always under attack, living in stress. How sad their success never really satisfies their souls!

In contrast, my Word tells you, "He who is willing to be a lowly servant is the greatest. And he is the one who succeeds in finding peace."

To the world this is the voice of utter madness. Irrelevant. But it is absolute, sublime truth. The few who follow me in this way of humble service find rest for their souls. They find that I actually do *save* them from terrible turmoil

... for they are no longer trapped in the struggle to surpass.

The same saving power is at work to deliver you from the guilt caused by the misdeeds of your past. No man, no woman is without a past. . . . The mistakes of youth, the vanity of glory-seeking, the hungry pursuit of empty pleasures, the unrestrained fantasies and outrageous behavior, the sowing of "wild oats"—all of it stains the soul, corrupts the character, defiles the body. And no one is exempt from these human experiences. Some may pretend to be perfect—but they are living behind a facade. They insist they have no need of a Savior.

On the other hand, when you turn to me in genuine remorse because of your misconduct . . . I am a strong deliverer! The moment you cry out, "Be merciful to me, a sinner!" I begin to respond. . . .

⸺∞⸺

I, the Friend of sinners, speak sweet solace to your spirit: "My son . . . my daughter . . . be at peace. Your sins are forgiven!"

What freedom from the guilt of the past! I tell you, "Your sins are remembered no more."

As your Savior, my infinite grace pours out to set you free from guilt . . . free to follow me in gratitude. Learning to live in freedom is the seal of your salvation. For as your Savior, I am committed to you—at work to re-create you in character and conduct. I am able to construct something new and strong and worthwhile from a destructive past. I am able to bring the brightest light of joy where there has been darkest despair. I redeem all the empty, pointless pursuits of your past. Instead of the wretched harvest fields that the locusts of lawless behavior have ruined, I birth in you new life . . . with bountiful years ahead.

All this is possible because I come to reside with you. I transform, reshape, and re-create a new character in you, akin to my own character. This new growth occurs day by day as you quietly allow my character to work in you.

All I ask from you, my child, is your calm compliance with my simple commands. Carry them out quietly and you will find supreme contentment. Trust me to work wonders in your life—I always do!

You will be astonished to find that you are really *free*—not only from the futility of your old life, but also from the folly of your old *self*, and your self-centeredness.

Being saved from the dreadful despair of self preoccupation is a glorious deliverance. Most people do not realize they are indeed their own worst enemy. They are so chained to their own desires. They do not understand how they struggle to satisfy their own selfish impulses. They labor under the load of self-gratification—an unrelenting bondage.

Over and over, I invite the worn and weary to come to me and find rest for their souls . . . along with new zest for abundant living.

I am the Savior who says, "I long to live my life in you day by day. You must determine to live out your life in me, hour by hour."

For my part . . . I am steadfast to carry out all of my eternal commitments to you. On your part . . . you must choose to carry out my commands in loyal devotion, confident that I can care for you completely.

Simply, do whatever I direct you to do. Learn to say "yes" to my wishes, and "no" to your old inclinations and desires. The instant you do this you find both my energy and my faith is given to you to live in freedom from your old nature. From a revengeful spirit, I save you to do good to those who despise and misuse you. From a quick-fire, reactive defensiveness, I save you to calmly respond as I would respond. From a sick soul that falls into every wallow of sin, I save you to triumph over every snare of sin in this world. I can empower you, so you no longer need to be a victim.

It is my saving presence that
provides your power
supplies your peace
insures your purity
and always prevails.

But to know the fullness of your salvation you cannot live independent of me. That is to live a lie, and I have no part in it. Here are the fundamental facts of our life together.

It takes two to be friends. Friendship works both ways. Friends have close communion. Friends have common interests. Friends find great delight in each other's company. Friends make much time to be together. Friends are loyal.

I am your Friend.

I am your Savior! I set you free to follow me: Follow and I set you free ... and keep you free....

Read, reflect, and in faith respond to:

Luke 2:1–20
Colossians 2:13–15
Psalms 51; 57
Isaiah 43:1–7
Mark 2:1–12
2 Corinthians 5:14–21
Philippians 2:1–15
Matthew 5:43–48
Joshua 1:9

9

"I Am Joy"

To those who receive me as Savior ... there is the discovery of great joy. Joy comes because they find me, and I am joy.

The joy I speak of is a dimension of my own being—distinct from what you call happiness. So many pursue happiness with a hungry passion. They have been deluded to believe that happiness lies buried at the foot of a rainbow. And like a rainbow, the elusive happiness of the world vanishes in a moment, leaving only clouds of disillusionment behind.

Human happiness is at best temporary, transient, tantalizing. It is utterly unpredictable, dependent on changing circumstances and the fluctuations of fickle human behavior.

If things are going well people appear to be happy.

If things are going wrong people become unhappy.

In large measure, human happiness depends upon your private emotional response to the outer circumstances of life. Whatever your senses interpret as "good" determines your inner state. This explains why so few are ever completely free from anxiety. It explains the endless search for safety and satisfaction that drives so many—even those who appear to have found success. This is not happiness, but an endless treadmill of escapism....

—⦿—

In contrast to the deceptive illusion of human happiness ... there flows steadily, surely, through all the universe a deep river of my joy. Its current brings refreshment, pure power, enthusiasm, enduring hope, buoyant good cheer....
Its fountainhead is found in me alone.

Find your joy in me—for I do not change. I am life and joy unceasing. To find your life in me is to find a celebration.

To know me as I am—unchanging—is to find your way into the supernatural dimension of life. Life that is *above* all natural life, not under its dominion. To know me as I am—unchanging—brings new enthusiasm into your daily experiences. For *enthusiasm* comes from the expression *en-theo*—meaning "in God." When your confidence is *in me* you share my life, my joy, my strength. Then nothing in the world can steal your joy.

When you come to know me in person, inner joy springs up from within your spirit. It is not a fleeting feeling, stirred up by your senses. It is an inner river of pure serene power that pervades you, from my presence. I give the assurance that I am with you. In this knowing you find you can rejoice in me no matter how difficult the circumstances of your life may be.

My child, the wobbly old world around you will be astonished by the manner in which my joy gives you such stability. You will not be tossed about by the changing conditions around you. You will not be dismayed by disappointments. Your inner strength has its source in me. What pure joy!

Approach me now. I am easy to approach. Come to me ... trusting ... and there will be a release of steady joy, from heaven to you.

Drink from this wondrous experience of joy within your own soul. It becomes a light, drawing others around you. You will experience the intense awareness that I come not to condemn but to set you free.

As you go on to walk with me gently, in ever more intimate communion, you will find deep, unshakable, profound joy in my presence with you. Unlike human happiness, so easily dismayed or shattered by circumstances, my joy prevails over the adversities of your life. Because I am here. I am with you. I am your joy amid every circumstance you encounter.

I wish to convey to you clearly the inner secret for the tremendous spiritual power expressed in my joy....

My beloved, a large part of our joy lies in the increasing realization ... which enfolds your soul ... that *I am yours, and you are mine—always!* There is enormous energy in this exchange of life between us. Sense ... and know ...

and rejoice in the truth ... that you are of great worth because you belong to me.

For me, there is ever-increasing joy in seeing your potential perfected in my presence. Day by day, month upon month, you are being changed from glory to glory, from weakness to strength of character, by our constant companionship.

In this supernatural transformation lies your marvelous and rock-solid *hope*. Not some wishful thinking, but the unshakable assurance that in my joy you can succeed ... you can find and live out my purposes.

In joy, find that purpose ... for you.

In the razzle-dazzle world, where so much emphasis is placed upon *the big show*, I call to you, my child: "Live quietly in deep joy and high hope." You need never be ashamed to tell anyone, anywhere about my loyalty and my love for you. For I am your joy. I am your hope. I am the secret to your tranquility in a troubled world.

Like a bird that sings bravely in the darkness, long before the dawn, so you too can be jubilant in the darkest hours—confident of my presence. Your buoyant optimism will not come from yourself ... it will come from me.

In this way, and only in this way, can you experience my abundant life. As my Life is your life, there flows from you a refreshing river that renews every life you touch.

The hallmark of your character and your conduct as my child will be the brightness of joy.

In simple sincerity, ask me to impart my Life to you daily. Open up your soul and spirit to receive me; I always come in ... and where I am there is unending joy!

Read, reflect, and in faith respond to:

Matthew 6:23–34; 28:20
Psalms 16:1–11; 43:1–5
Isaiah 55:1–13
Joshua 1:1–9
Luke 15:1–7, 11–32
John 15:7–11
Hebrews 12:1–4

10

"I Am Faithful"

I am faithful
in all my ways
in all your days
in all my Word says.
I am absolutely steadfast
absolutely secure
absolutely sure.

You can find no other who can make such claims in all of the universe. Only I endure throughout eternity.

All else is transient. Everyone else is subject to change. Though I tell mankind this eternal truth a thousand times, from generation to generation ... only a few turn me, only a few trust me above all else. This is because you are locked inside time and space. Even your most brilliant scientists and scholars forget that fundamental fact. Many behave as though they have unraveled the mysteries of the cosmos—while missing the greatest mystery of time and eternity! Nothing less than my faithfulness, in all that I am, all that I do.

Were it not for my faithfulness, present and undeviating in the design of everything, the physical world would disintegrate in disarray. There would be no law, no order, no design, no beauty, no balance.

Behind the scenes of every process at work in your world, screened from your eyes by your fallen nature, my infallible faithfulness goes on. And so, men grope around in the darkness of lower, fleshly perceptions until the time comes when they turn to me.

Sometimes I cause your "real" world to let you down, so that you will look beyond it, and find me....

⊗⊗⊗

I am faithful ... because I reside in eternal illumination. In me there is no darkness at all. In my presence there is no despair. I am beyond all deception. In me there is no decadence. So I am utterly reliable in all my ways.

This is the basis upon which I can invite all men, women, and children to come to me ... to invest their faith in me. For, you see my precious child, I am safe and steady ground on which your soul can stand.

Trust me only a little. Just *try* me—and you will know why you need only a small amount of faith to discover my surety. Even a "mustard seed" of faith will prove my faithfulness.

For nothing depends, ultimately, on you. It is my faith-fulness that
    validates your faith in me
    vindicates your faith in me
    makes you victorious over the world system.

Child ... I call you child, urging you to live by child-like faith in me. I am your faithful Father, and I reach out to take hold of your searching soul. I extend to you un-failing care.

Only accept my offer, if you wish to enjoy my bene-fits.... Do not trust in your money more than me. Do not rely on your guns more than my greatness. Do not invest your faith in human skills more than my wisdom. This is all a great grief to me.

I come, and come, and come to troubled people in their turmoil and tension. I offer myself as their surety. But many prefer to place confidence in other people—they choose to trust almost anyone else *but* me. Though I come looking for faith, I find so little....

Those of you who will dare to trust me, you are sur-prised at the serenity that confidence in me brings. Ab-solute trust is one of the supreme secrets to finding rest for your souls and repose for your spirits. The assurance that "all is well" for I am here transcends all of your trou-bles and enables you to triumph over every adversity. This is more than high-sounding phrases—it can be your daily delight when you trust me! But there is a barrier....

Instead of standing firm in living faith in me, so many choose to live in the realm of their feelings. Don't you see?—Your emotions are mostly natural responses to all the observable events, circumstances, and human relationships that affect your existence. In fact, this is a very shallow, turbulent, and uncertain way in which to deal with the turmoil of your time on earth. It means you live only on the basis of what you *see, hear, touch, taste,* or *smell,* with your five fallible, physical senses. Allowing your emotions to be governed and conditioned by these natural phenomena is known as "living by sight."

I call you to live by faith in me. This faith that I ask you to exercise is a supernatural capacity that comes from me and is grounded in my faithfulness to you. I share it with every soul, so all men have faith. Their problem is to discover the supreme object in which to rest their faith.

There are a few things on which people rest their faith ...

> education and science
> > business transactions
> government programs
> > health schemes
> human skills and expertise
> > church activities
> family and friends.

None of these is essentially evil but all are transient. Every one fluctuates, changes, and can easily delude you. Only I remain forever faithful.

It is to a life of complete confidence in my character that I invite you. Do not be afraid to trust me though you cannot see or touch me. For I assure you I never leave. I am with you to the end of your days on earth ... and on into eternity.

In earth, there is no greater guarantee. Faith in me is the absolute assurance for your soul. Just calmly come and trust me.

Invest your faith in me from now on.

I am forever faithful.

It takes a clear decision of your intellect to make the reasonable choice. Everything in your will must be brought into it!

What you invest your faith in is the supreme spiritual issue of eternity. Faith is not a matter of sensual emotion to be indulged in at the moment. A superficial, ecstatic experience does not endure. Too often "religious emotions" are triggered by sensational stories, soft music, and the stimulus of massed crowds. I deal with you privately, personally creating truly changed lives. When I call you to come to me, you *will* experience genuine contrition of spirit and deep repentance—whether you feel emotion or not.

I call you, quite simply, from trusting in transient things.

I call you, instead, to turn and trust in me by faith.

I am faithful to give you faith to do this.

I am the One who honors your faith.

You begin to live in my faith.

This is my Life in you.

I am both the Author and Finisher of your faith.

Author and Finisher,

I am the Creator of your faith.

I am the Living Christ who conveys to you my faith in the Father.

I am the Constant Companion who exercises my faith in you.

I am the Supreme Savior who honors and vindicates this supernatural faith in your affairs.

For you to live in faith, my beloved, is to live without foreboding and without fear. It is to stand on a Rock of superb confidence amid chaos. You are able to live in triumph.

Always, this has been one of my supreme purposes for you—to be a victor, not a victim. To be valiant and courageous, for I am faithful.

———∞———

I honor your smallest investment of trust at once. I actually step into your life day by day. You find that you are given the will, the determination, the firm resolve to do my work gladly. The instant you step out with the calm confidence that I will achieve my purposes for you, you are empowered with the supernatural energy of my Spirit.

This happens as harmony and mutual goodwill grows between us. You are lead by my Spirit, and energized by my presence—even in the most mundane events of your life. Your calm and serene attitude of determined dependence on me injects enormous strength into your life. You are set free from fear, foreboding, and fretting.

If you reflect on this, my child, you will realize how different the life of *faith* is from living by *sight*. What a contrast between those two lifestyles!

Those who base their lives only on observable facts will always remain far from me. Such a person may be convinced they know the right way to proceed. Their life seems so proper and sophisticated. Yet it is the path of enormous peril, and ends in spiritual death.

When the twelve Israelite spies went into Canaan to reconnoiter the land, they did not trust in me. Instead they determined to gather all the "data"—and most came back utterly confused. This created foreboding, great fear, and ultimate failure to fully take the territory I had promised them. Only my stalwarts—Joshua and Caleb—were men of calm faith. Because they stood upon my faithfulness to them, they alone entered into the rich territory and took it in my strength. The ten who were merely fact-finders, who lived by sight, died in the desert.

Live by faith in me, and take tremendous territory in my authority. I do not lead you into tough situations and challenging encounters to frighten you. I am faithful to you, my friend, as you follow me. I purposely take you into new and exciting territory to prove my invincible faithfulness—no matter where we go together!

You, too, can triumph over trouble.

You, too, can take new terrain in my name.

You, too, can enjoy remarkable repose in my company.

Cast the full weight of your whole life onto my faithfulness. You will be amazed ... for life with me becomes a grand adventure!

Read, reflect, and in faith respond to:

Joshua 1:1–9
Colossians 1:9–22
John 1:1–14
Matthew 17:14–21
Romans 12:1–3
Galatians 2:19–20
Luke 17:11–19
I Corinthians 2:1–16
Numbers 13:17–30; 14:1–11

11

"I Am Good"

*I*n the world, the concept most people have of me is the *opposite* of absolute reality.

Whenever there is a natural disaster that destroys property and takes lives, people shout, "This is an act of God!" Hurricanes, killer earthquakes, titanic floods, volcanic devastation—anything that brings destruction and death is said to be my fault. Your "wise ones," seeking to blame someone for the calamities of earth decide to lay blame on me. Yet in the same breath, these skeptics cynically deny I exist! If, as they claim, "God is dead!" how can I be so busy and creative in destruction?

Little wonder there is such confusion in the council

chambers of the "wise." No marvel that there is such mayhem among you. Not surprising that human behavior is so bizarre.

The single greatest reason for all the folly of human affairs is the false perception people have of my character. Most regard me as a terrible monster. They suppose I reside somewhere out in the cold regions of space, that I look down upon the world and its people with a perverse, malicious attitude. They think I find sick delight in bringing disaster and death to your race.

Am I making this up? Consider all the vicious "gods" and despicable "deities" that have been devised by your religious leaders. For thousands of years human cultures have lived in terror of false gods, evil spirits, and dark deities who held them in deception and despair. *All because men believed God was evil.*

Quite the opposite!

I am good!

I am always good!

I am essentially good!

―◦∞◦―

All that I am is good. Goodness itself.

All that I do, all that I declare is for your good. In my mercy toward you, my kindness for you, my long-suffering among you, my ultimate goodwill is at work.

Most men and women have no idea that it is possible to find the *supreme good* in this life. There may be silent, intense moments of great poignancy within the soul, when the inner man yearns for this supreme good—but at best they are fleeting wisps that blow away, leaving an aching void of emptiness.

Yet I am the *supreme good.* Come to *me.* Meet *me.* Know

me. Experience goodness from hour to hour. Enjoy a bountiful life with me. All because I am good.

But do not misunderstand. . . .

The good life I offer is not one of selfish, extravagant luxuries. Not the ease and wealth that worldly people call "the good life." Rather, it is *above* the pressure to have money, things, and the envy of other people. *This* kind of life and my life are poles apart!

I call you into my good life—which is the laying aside of a life that looks for fleshly gratification, the stimulation of fleshly senses. It is a life lived *above* the senses in which *grace* is your life. My life in you is your life. Poured through you for your good and the good of others.

Of course you can live out your life under the dominion of a world that has "gone wrong" . . . a world drowning in an increasing flood of filth, corruption, and perversion. You can choose to live in a world where every man worships his own version of god. But gods created by the fallen minds of men are always going to be a moral cancer in civilization. Every society in which men have created hosts of false gods to worship has collapsed, pitching nations into chaos.

Do you see? The same pattern is repeated whenever men and women repudiate my goodness. Whenever they choose to indulge their own selfish and wicked ways and call it *god.*

In the end each person, each community, each culture accepts or rejects the goodness that I offer. That is why I have said that you must choose—whether to be for me or against me. . . . Always, I have been despised and rejected by the majority and loved by a few who are my true friends.

Good
eternal good
divine good
my good
always polarizes people.
The enormous energy evident in my goodness antagonizes all who are evil. The two forces are ever in open conflict: Though I did nothing but good among men, still you chose to attack me—and even crucify me in utter humiliation!

Do you think you know what the good life is? How to choose between good and evil? Apart from me you cannot choose *good*. For evil that lies in the very nature of human behavior despises good. Debauchery hates honor. The corrupt hate those who are truly noble.

Choose me—for I will have the last word in the horrendous horror of human history. My good triumphs over evil in the end. It is always so.

After darkness, light comes. . . .

———

At the hour of my death, terrifying darkness descended over the earth. Darkness quenched light. Evil silenced good. Men fed the darkness with their sneers. Spitting in my face, they spat in the face of God. Driving spikes of iron through my hands and feet, plunging a spear into my side—they murdered goodness.

But after the cruel cross, my eternal Spirit burst free!—free to pour out full forgiveness to all men of all time.

Because I mastered the darkness of pain and death—and it did not master me—I have the authority to bring never-ending good to all who are sunk down in the darkness of sin, set against me. How is this so?

I ask you to do only this to win over all darkness: Exchange your life for my life. Exchange your eyes of *flesh* for eyes of *faith* and see me as the One who governs your life—every event—in goodness. Exchange your heart—which is full of fear that you will lose something dear to you in this world—for a heart that is alive in the hope of eternity where nothing can be lost and all is restored.

You will experience a majestic mystery when you make this titanic transaction. You will find my life in a way that transcends all human thought. In this way you come alive to my Spirit, and the darkness and deeds of the flesh lose their hold. For I caused Christ, who himself knew nothing of sin, to be sin for your sake, so that in Christ you might be made good with the goodness of God. See how high I am in goodness, with the eyes of faith, and I will show you how low are the sinful things that draw you by their false promises of life. My spirit will assimilate your evil desires and, in exchange, impart to you my great good.

This exchange is offered freely to all fallen men and women. For I have accomplished absolute victory over every evil—even the entrenched selfishness of human nature.

Give me all of yourself. Take my goodness in place of your evil. Take my character and my honorable ways in place of your shame and tendency to conceal wrongdoing.

I am the One for whom your soul hungers and thirsts. Only in me will you find satisfaction. Taste of my life, and know that I am good. Never will you hunger and thirst for anything in the world again.

Let me breathe into you, to inspire your spirit. Trust

me—when I stir your soul with the shakings I allow in your life—to undergird you with courage and strength to follow me in unflinching faith. This is what it means to actually share in my life from above.

You see, my goodness is not a sweet, fragile *idea*—it is the power of my presence as I fight in you to conquer the awfulness of sin *in your experiences.* It is my Person at work in you, defeating all the evil that assails you, making you victorious in spirit. It is the revealing of my *purpose* for you, dispelling your despair. My goodness defeats your despondency and gives new hope for the days ahead.

My goodness, which the world maligns, is in fact the force that counteracts all corruption in the cosmos. Corruption of any sort has never triumphed over me. Above all pain, sin, heartache, and death—I rise in power! I rise in purity . . . and in peace! I rise to proclaim to all men that they can enter the spiritual kingdom where my goodness reigns by choosing to make the leap of faith.

I invite you now to choose: Does evil have final authority? Or can you have faith and trust that my goodness wins in the end, in *all* things?

When you enter my kingdom by faith, my goodness will give you
noble purposes
strong character
wholesome attitudes
reliable conduct
integrity
shining goodwill.
And I must tell you about the inevitable consequences. . . .

The man or woman who stands up for me and has faith in my goodness—they will not be popular! Those around you will either be attracted or repelled by my good and evident work in you. Many will be uncomfortable in your company.

There is a high price to pay.

So many are sure that goodness is nothing but a dull grind. They are deluded, and think that a good person is a bore. They find perverse pleasure in persecuting those who are pure, noble, upright, and honorable. How wrong.

But be of great good cheer. In this world you will encounter tribulation—but I have overcome it all! So can you, as I live in you.

My good will prevail: Live in hope of the new day, when goodness will dawn again. Look up, and be glad in me.

Read, reflect, and in faith respond to:

Psalm 53:1–6
Jeremiah 4:17–31; 9:23–24; 29:11–14
Matthew 12:30–37; 25:31–46
2 Timothy 3:1–7
Romans 12:9–21
2 Corinthians 5:14–21
Isaiah 55:1–13
John 16:33

12

"I Am Love"

*I*n the realm of humanity, no other concept is given
more attention than *love*. *Love* inspires thousands of
songs and ballads. Love is the thread of emotional tension
that runs through many books. Love is depicted everywhere in art ... discussed *ad nauseam* in the media. It is
perverted in private discussions. Special courses in love are
offered by so-called "specialists" who really know little
about it. Love is preached from pulpits.

But no other word is more abused, more misunder-
stood.

I am Love.

I am not weak, soft, or sentimental in my love. My love

springs from my eternal nature so that it overcomes every obstacle as I seek to draw all men to me . . . and into me.

What I want to tell you now can change your view of me . . . and change *you* forever.

———⊗⊗⊗———

I am Love. All true love has its source in the fountainhead of my love.

I brought mankind into being. I gave you the capacity to express and receive love, in all its forms. I intended that love should motivate and empower you toward good and lofty living. In man's arrogance, some spurn this view of high and pure love. They accept lower views.

Let me tell you about love. . . .

———⊗⊗⊗———

Love finds expressions in three ways:

First, in erotic love, which fulfills the sensual needs of the body.

Second, in filial love, which fulfills the soul's need for the loyalty and companionship of family and friends.

Third, in godly love—my love—which fulfills your spirit's need for a benefactor who is not limited to time and earthly circumstances.

From the beginning of time, men and women have felt a desire to dwell together in the harmony of a home. The two were to be bound together into a single unit by sexual satisfaction and the procreation of children. These little ones were intended to flourish and thrive in the safety of faithful family ties. In this beautiful environment, the expression of sexual love between loyal parents is to this day a wonderful passion.

You cannot know the grief I hold in my Spirit as, all over the earth, this lofty plan is destroyed. For many, sexual desire has been debased into selfish exploitation of others. Eroticism, narcissism, fornication, gross brutality, pornography, abortion, homosexuality—all are "legitimized" in the name of freedom.

Next, there is the great capacity I bestowed on human beings to express loving loyalty to each other. Such filial love was to fan out from families to embrace friends and associates whose lives are touched while traveling down life's tangled trails. You cannot know my deep dismay as I look upon your world where the fabric of friendship is torn by disloyalty.

As fallen mankind moves farther from my purposes in these two kinds of love you will see
broken hearts
broken homes
broken hopes
broken promises
broken families
broken friendships
broken children.
Do you wonder that I look upon the world ... and weep?

Many will try to tell you that these sexual aberrations are merely "games." They are deadly and destroy the human soul. Self-centered indulgence is not "liberation." It is slavery, and the end result is emptiness and death. Death to love itself.

I, the source of love, cry out to you: Turn from your loveless ways! I plead with you: Repent of your wrongs before your soul is ruined beyond temptation! Listen to my warning and choose the Life I give you from above— rather than the flesh and death.

This choice is yours to make. You can enter into a new life of love as I teach you what true love is.

The love I demonstrated when I came to you....

———⊗⊗⊗———

I could have *told* you about love. I chose to show you my love, so that you could see and hear and touch love— I came to you in the flesh. My love begins when one life is laid down for another. Even so, many despise and reject me—for *selfishness* resents *selflessness*.

When I say I am Love, I mean I am the love of God made known to all men. This love is always expressed, every day, in my life poured out for you, and you experience it when you gladly lay down your life for others.

In my love, I am
utterly selfless
self-sacrificing
self-giving.

To love as I love is to receive life and light and love, and to give out to others as I lead you. It begins as you trust me in the simplicity of a child. When you know my constant love for you, you can rest in me. Remember the supreme sacrifice I made for you on a bloodstained cross, and you will know I can never leave you ... never forsake you. My sacrifice—this was the only way your blinded souls could ever perceive my love.

Such wondrous love is foreign to mankind. Because it is beyond human behavior, it is considered almost bizarre. Human pride will not accept such an outpouring of love from another. Most people cannot believe it is offered freely. They would prefer to earn it, or repay it with their own efforts—a thin veil over their hidden pride.

Just now ... in this moment ... lay down your pride, and accept into yourself a love that you cannot earn....

Nothing you can do, nothing you can offer, will buy my love.... I love you!

And my supreme desire is to bestow love upon you. Share in my love as you share in my life. Receive my love as you receive me. The joyful capacity to give my love, no matter what is said or done to you, comes as you live in my presence ... by my Spirit. My power energizes you to live in my love, and to live out my love to others. Think on these things....

My love is the dynamic that undergirds everything noble in your world. It proceeds from my grace, my goodness, my generosity to all men and women ... to all other living organisms in the universe. My love flows to

your own precious children
the fawn in the woods
the calf in the field
the fledgling in its nest.

I care for each one, and I sustain each one. Because I am, you live and grow within my love.

If I were to withdraw myself—my Spirit and power—the earth would disintegrate. You can glimpse this fact in the lives of those who deliberately—in arrogance, pride, and folly—shut me out of their souls. Their end is utter ruin and dreadful despair. They go out into darkness and ultimate death—and they do so because they choose to deny themselves my love, and prefer to degenerate until their souls are destroyed.

Do you understand that I do not condemn any person? That each one chooses this awful self-annihilation? By their own willful choice, they condemn themselves. In spite of such deliberate folly—and the world is filled with it— I come to everyone in my love. I call out to all in my compassion. I invite you to come to me and find new life.

Understand that my gracious Spirit, filled with love and grace, will not always strive with men and women. The day is rapidly approaching when the world's cup of iniquity and violence will be filled. Mankind will have chosen to satiate its soul in the dark wine of willful rebellion and outright rejection of my love for you. Then will come sudden destruction and utter ruin.

But this will not be so for you.

There is still hope for all who will turn to me and live in my love.

Will you call others to live in my love? Will you lead others into a life of love? The world is crying out for the love we can show them together.

My love pulverizes prejudice and builds enduring loyalty.

My love moves hearts to be generous, to serve and benefit others.

My love stirs hearts to pour out for the poor, the lonely, the sick.

My love sets hearts free from fear, anger, anxiety.

My love sets hearts free from the feverish drive to own and possess things that can never give life.

In me
in my love
in my life

you find abundant life, refreshing you with rest, permeated with profound peace, jubilant with joy. A great adventure.

I love you, my child!

Read, reflect, and in faith respond to:

I John 3:18
Genesis 6:5–13
Matthew 24:4–24
Isaiah 5:11–25
Deuteronomy 8:1–20
Romans 5:1–11
John 3:10–21

13

"I Am Peace"

*T*hroughout human history—so replete with hatred, cruelty, and suffering—I have come to you in peace. And yet the astonishing fact is that men often lay the blame for strife and war on me.

Most people are quick to blame someone else for their difficulties. That tendency has become more pronounced, as so-called experts in psychology and psychiatry have insisted no one is fully responsible for their misconduct. Is it any wonder that crime, genocide, and wars escalate all over the earth? While at the same time you cry out: "Peace—peace." But there is no peace. And in its place, only terror and atrocities.

The reason for this cruel conduct is man's essential *self-centeredness*. Each person insists on their own *rights*. This results in the inevitable clash of self-interests, confrontations, conflict, and chaos. Despite all the treaties and legal arrangements put in place to protect people, peace really does not prevail.

All over the world people plead for peace.

They plan peace conferences.

They prattle on and on about peace.

But they cannot find, in themselves, the secret of peace.

I will tell you why.

Men and women are at war within themselves. Their struggle spills out in constant conflict with others. And the real struggle is their rebellion against me.

This secret inner war complicates all human conduct. Corrupts all human culture. Corrodes all civilizations. It brings endless confusion upon the earth.

Brother rises against brother. Parents attack their own children. The world is set ... neighbor against neighbor ... community against community ... clan against clan ... nation against nation. Sorrow is heaped upon sorrow. Groans go up to me.

And I, the Prince of Peace, groan over your world.

Humanists and socialists propose a New World Order, thinking they can usher in a worldwide utopia. But it will never happen. Have you not witnessed awful atrocities by so-called "human saviors"? The truth is, men never learn much from the gruesome mistakes of their forebears, from one generation to the next.

You will not find a man-made formula for peace on

earth. But you can find a source of peace that comes from above the earth. . . .

❦

I am Peace. I can give you peace beyond human wisdom. The peace I give is not the sort the world offers you.

My peace is not passivity—not a complacent uninvolvement in the challenges of life.

On the contrary, the peace I produce pours out from my selfless, self-giving, self-forgetting, self-sacrificing offer of life—given freely even to my enemies. My love is laid out, even for my opponents. My presence gives serenity, strength, and stability in spite of every insult, every antagonism, every hatred.

So many do not even know that I do not come to you in anger, in hostility, in condemnation. I come in peace. I greet you in peace. I accept you in peace. I bless you in peace.

I am not at war with you. Yet many of you are at war with me.

You think this is not so?

When your personal dreams fail . . . when your self-centered plans and prayers come apart . . . when you envy and decide life is not fair . . . when another human being fails or hurts you . . . who do you accuse? You accuse, resent, and even rage at . . . *me*. And though you claim to know me, your soul continues at enmity with me.

Since your first war is with me, your first step on the road to peace is to make peace with me. . . .

❦

This is not the treaty I have made with you. I have

paid the price to set you free from anger, hostility, and hatred. I extend compassion, forgiveness, acquittal of all your wrongs . . . and total acceptance. This is the peace I offer you so we can begin to live in peace. It is my gift . . . in you and through you . . . to the world.

My treaty with the world is the presence of the Prince of Peace in your life.

My presence brings serenity of soul. Though all around you may be in tension or turmoil, deep within will lie the still waters of inner calm. Your thoughts will be tranquil, not turbulent. Your will need no longer pull you in every direction. For I lead you in the paths of peace, for your sake and as a witness to my honor.

This is the result when you accept the terms of my peace treaty. This is what it means to be saved in soul, saved from the trauma of your time, saved from a disintegrating world.

My beloved one, do not hesitate to lift your spirit to me, to delight in my presence. Relish the touch of peace as my Spirit comes to rest in you. It is my presence—my own Spirit within your spirit—that confirms you are indeed my child. Peace.

My presence speaks peace . . . makes peace . . . in your spirit.

My presence purges your conscience from all condemnation.

My presence provides you with the inner power to meet life in confidence.

My peace that surpasses all ordinary understanding is the knowledge of my presence with you, and within you. I find enormous pleasure in giving you my Spirit in this intimate manner. This is how you are meant to live with me—not in enmity, but in perpetual peace. I in you. You in me. But there is much more. . . .

—∞∞—

My peace will strengthen and heal your mortal body. For your body becomes my temple, my special sanctuary, when I am present with you.

When you become aware of my presence, resident within you, you will regard your body as more than merely a physical frame. You will understand it is a royal residence. This is the true honor I bestow on your body.

It is no longer yours alone, to do with as you choose. I brought it into being, and bought it with my laid-down life. I sustain all of its actions by my might. I provide for its health and healing.

My child, do not abuse or neglect the body we share. Be responsible to serve as a proper caretaker of my residence. Keep your body pure, clean, healthy, fit for my occupancy. Never pollute, defile, or neglect my royal residence. Do not war against your own body.

Do I not come to you in peace, and purity? Your part is to keep a proper place for me. Your entire being—soul, spirit, body—can be made clean. The impact of my peaceful presence can begin a full re-creation.

Throw open all the doors, and let me come in like a mighty rushing wind! Let me drive out all the dust, debris, and pollution of your past . . . every area in which we have lived in conflict. Come to peace.

—∞∞—

Who will listen to me? Who will fully accept my treaty

of peace? Who will lay down all striving to have me within?

You say you want peace. But only when your ways conform to my plan will peace be yours. Then even your enemies will be kept at peace with you.

Is your mind an enemy to you? Your emotions? Your body? Your parent, child, or spouse? Your neighbor? Have you lost a friend?

Come to me, and take my peace. Let peace rule *in* you . . . and peace will pour out *from* you.

Make no mistake, though.

Inevitably, when you share my life, you will be scorned and rejected by many. They will call you a fool for becoming, like me, a person of peace. For I did good, and still I was hated. It will be the same for you. For

evil rejects good

the beast despises beauty

selfishness loathes selflessness.

But you . . . you be a person of peace!

Though someone raises a conflict with you, be at peace with them. Overcome evil with good. Turn from conflict to peace—turn to me—and we will prevail over every adversary. My life, my energy, my goodwill surmounts every obstacle. My peace presses on in good cheer. Open yourself to me in every conflict, and a remarkable peace will flood your character, your actions, and even the caliber of your conversation.

Peace, goodwill, good cheer, strength of spirit, and serenity of soul—these will replace animosity, bitterness, hostility, anger, jealousy, and quarreling. My life can be exchanged for your old ways in every encounter. You are re-created in peace, and out of this exchange will come great healing to the world.

Here are the steps you need to take in order to enter into my presence . . . and my peace.

Face your own failings squarely. Do not try to cover up your own inclinations to fight, argue, defend, and attack. Do not cover up your belligerence with lame excuses. Instead, earnestly cast yourself upon me in genuine contrition. Cry out to me: "Prince of Peace, fill my mind, my emotions, my will so that I love as you love. Help me to give myself in peace to others, as you give yourself in peace to me."

I will answer your cry! By my presence, through my Spirit, your self-protective pride will be replaced with self-giving strength. Your ill-will can be refashioned into my goodwill.

Know me in humility, and you will live in peace ... with me, with yourself, and with others.

———

Walk the path of peace. And in time you will grow strong in me. You will grow calm under my control. You will be changed ... into a person of peace.

Read, reflect, and in faith respond to:

James 4:1–10
John 14:23–31; 20:18–33
Philippians 4:3–9
Romans 8:9–21
Hebrews 4:9–16
I Corinthians 3:16–21
Proverbs 16:1–9
Matthew 5:43–48

14

"I Am Moderation"

*T*hrough galaxies and star systems ... in all the affairs of men and angels ... all the biota on earth ... there is an amazing *influence of order.*

That is because I am the eternal One, who controls the cosmos, who brings balance to all that exists. I am the One who exercises *moderation* over all.

In all the universe only I am consistent. I am beautifully balanced. All else swings from extreme to extreme. But there are no crises with me!

You say, "If anything more can go wrong, it will!" But the *disorder* is all in your bewildered, blinded worldview. Come to me, and I will show you all in my perspective.

Come to me and get knowledge and understanding. Then you will not only perceive all things in balance, you will be able to maintain moderation and balance in what you do and say. That is, you will no longer be governed by stray whims, and by circumstances that seem to career into you out-of-control. You will understand that everything is moderated—governed—by me.

———⊗⊗⊗———

I determine the destiny of all things.

You are not the master of your own destiny. Some believe they are, and in the end this view leads many to self-destruct. The path of personal pride and power, which many choose, is deadly. Pride precedes a fall. Power leads to corruption. Prestige ends in self-delusion. And still, so many wish to seize full control of their own affairs. They are determined to do their own thing, even if it leads to ruin and remorse. *Anything* . . . rather than accept my rule over their lives!

Men pride themselves on discovering "secrets" of time management, money-management, assertiveness—confident that learning these skills will give them the power they crave to control their own lives and determine their own destiny. But as a result, they are forever fraught with anxiety over the unknown future, caught up in "success" and the pursuit of pleasures that lead only to soul-deadening boredom.

The words "Vanity of vanity, all is vanity" came from the soul of a man who lived life to its absolute extremes. Everything the world could offer Solomon he indulged in to the limit: wealth, women, wine; power, prestige, pride; fame, fortune, fun—Solomon consumed them all to the full. There was no balance to his behavior. No self-control.

Though he could have become the greatest monarch to reign under my control, he chose to pursue his own perverse path. And the end of it was emptiness and cynicism.

The world is full of "Solomons"—men and women who are wise in their own eyes. And in life they are called upon to make thousands of decisions. Their lives become the product of their choices.

Most prefer to go it on their own. Insisting on their own way, their own rights, they have made a chaos of conflict and confrontation in human society.

Consequently, legislators enact law after law in a vain attempt to bring balance, decency, and order into your society—all in an attempt to protect one person from being preyed upon by another—but lawlessness goes on and on. Some sneer, "You cannot legislate morality." Your courts are a battleground of litigation, where lawyers earn incredible fees to settle suits for rage that is out of control. And the victims of crime still suffer greater loss than the criminals themselves. . . .

The terrible truth is, the chaos and pain will increase because you refuse to turn over the control to me: I am moderation.

<hr />

Inviting you, my beloved, to come under my control does not mean that I am inviting you to a life of ease, wherein you become a puppet in my hand. I tell you in truth, that the trail of life we shall walk together will have its tears. It will have its thorns and its dark days. But every step of the way I will hold your hand and guide you securely. Together we will govern your soul in strength and peace. Together we will triumph over the chaos that seeks to consume you.

I can master any force—within you or without you—no matter how powerfully chaotic it seems.

My earthly life has often been regarded with dismay by historians, scholars, and academics who have only worldly wisdom. In their ignorance they assume I was a victim of circumstances. Some say I was a misguided zealot for whom things went terribly wrong and thus my life ended in disaster. Just the opposite is true! All that I did and said—from birth to death to resurrection to ascension—was under my Father's control. I demonstrated in human form what it means to live in supernatural moderation.

As a result, the grace of God was poured out—everlasting life has spilled from the portals of heaven to millions upon millions throughout history.

Do you see it? The work I did was also my Father's work. Every word I spoke, every act I did was one piece of a plan that far outlasted my life on earth.

This is what I invite you to: A life lived within the Father's grand design; a life of meaning and purpose; a life that is under control, because it is lived in my control; a life *fulfilled*.

Yes, it is entirely possible for you, an ordinary person, to live an extraordinary life. One of composure, self-control, and quiet assurance in a world gone chaotic. You can be a beautifully balanced human being, not given to fear or folly amid all the mayhem—all through the faith I impart to you daily.

Trust me *fully*, and you will not be shaken by adversity. You will abide in my Word to you: It will abide in you, for I am in you to sustain you.

Some may sneer at the new balance and moderation in you, because of their spiritual blindness. They cannot see that you are under my constant care. I am your Counselor.

Under my care you can be a consistent conqueror.

I do not *remove* obstacles from your path and cover it with rose petals, but I promise to pour out my power, patience, and peace within you. You will triumph over trouble and rise in newness of life; you will turn tragedy into eternal triumph.

Will you place every piece of your life under my care ... and my control?

———— ∞∞∞ ————

My child, I call to you earnestly! Set your *will*. Choose to turn over the whole of your "self" to my control: All your

    appetites
    drives
    instincts
    and desires

can be brought into harmony with my highest purpose for you. It also means you can live a noble life of moderation and temperance, even in the most fiery testing.

Live calmly and simply in me. You will discover that your self-control enables others around you to sense my peace and calm through you. It spills from me through you—and you become part of my supreme plan to help preserve a perishing world. This inner peace and outer power come at a high cost—a price that few are not willing to pay.

The price is this: You must sacrifice your personal rights to my service—to my plan to extend my loving rule over all the earth.

Decide to give up your self-rule, and turn yourself over—*irrevocably*—to me. This decisive self-relinquishment is like a mountain climber who finally passes over the great divide and starts down the shining snow slopes on the other side. There is no turning back. No return to the old struggle to surpass. Just a smooth, swift passage now into new terrain, taking over new territory. . . . Where I guide you, go, taking great strides, seeing wide new vistas stretch away to new horizons.

You discover what it is to be set free at last. Free from
the stifling atmosphere of self-interest
the shackles of self-importance and insecurity
the struggle to impress others
the feverish scramble to succeed
the sinister grip of selfish vanity.

Free to live contentedly under my control. For I long for my children to share my power—the power that can reshape society.

What I am calling you to should not daunt you. My work is not done in a day. Rather, it is a life of stirring adventure that unfolds week by week, year after year. Do not hesitate to turn to me each day to discover my intentions for you as they are revealed in the details of your daily experience.

Do you want to know me, in an intimacy that surpasses any human companionship? Do you want to find me closer, more compatible, than any mortal companion? You will never be abandoned to chaos if you allow me to share your life.

Choose my moderation and
little by little
step by step
moment by moment
you will know superb satisfaction as I regulate your life in concord with my great plan. My governing presence will bring great changes in your character. The old passions and the formidable pride that enslaved your soul will pass away.

In their place will come pure motives and a humble heart that I can direct. For humility is my hallmark.

I, the eternal One, the Most High Majesty, find enormous pleasure in close communion with you. My Spirit moves relentlessly all over the earth . . . searching . . . seeking for anyone who will relinquish their rights and accept my supreme sovereignty. Few indeed accept the rest that comes from submitting to my control.

But if *you* decide to do so . . .

You will discover a wondrous dimension of my love that will energize you beyond imagination! Wherever you are, whatever your part in my plan, I am there to accomplish wondrous things through you. A person under my control is a formidable force for constructive change. *You* can be that person. *You* can make a difference in a dying world.

As you live simply in my care, you will enable others simply to live.

Read, reflect, and in faith respond to:

Job 42:1–6
Ecclesiastes 1:1–11
Deuteronomy 11:16–28
Philippians 2:1–13
John 17:1–26
Ephesians 3:9–21
Luke 9:23–26
2 Corinthians 2:14–17; 3:17–18

15

"I Am the Way"

I am the Way."
Such a simple statement.

Four words—but they reveal the most profound truth ever spoken. They are my eternal assurance to you.

I am the Way—the only way whereby a person can comprehend the marvelous character of God.

I am the only way in which any seeking soul can find the essential glory and grace of the eternal One.

I am the only way that anyone can discover firsthand something of the love I have for you.

I am the only way you will experience full forgiveness for all your faults.

I am the only way you are delivered from spiritual death to eternal life.

I am the way of hope ... the way of light ... companionship ... enduring peace ... satisfaction ... strength.

Exchange your life for my life, and all these spiritual transformations will flourish in you as you grow in my presence. My Way is transformation.

I am the Way ... of care.

You were brought into being to know my care for you. For I am yours and you are mine!

This is the supreme secret of the ages: I in you and you in me. An eternal, enduring exchange of your emptiness and need for my fullness and care.

You were brought into being to be my child.

I entered your world to become your Father. Only in giving yourself to One who is greater and more glorious than yourself can you find supreme satisfaction.

Give me all of yourself and I will begin to give you myself. That is the way I am. Enter into my eternal care, and my care will enter into you.

My way is security beyond anything the world can offer.

I am the Way ... of intimate knowing.

To know me, you must live in me. When you live in me you will love me. You can never be disappointed when you live your smaller life within my greater life. I am the way to life everlasting. And I am the way to abundant life on earth.

My way is enthusiastic life with profound purpose, here and now.

⸺⸺

Many assume wrongly that I am only the God of heaven . . . the God of *later* . . . the God of the afterlife. That is a serious misunderstanding. My Way is the Way of honor and exuberance on earth for your life—now. Few know about this way of living, simply because they do not know me. They have not yet learned what it means
to live with me
to love me fervently
to be loyal to me.
Claiming they know me, they live as strangers to me! I do not tell you this to be harsh, but to correct you. For I stretch out my arms to all people, inviting them to come and walk in my way . . . surrender to my life. But most prefer to pursue their own paths, perilous as they may be!

Here is a true word: One of the great secrets to life is not always to do what you like—but always to like what you do.

Am I not the one who—more than *anyone* else—knows precisely what you are best suited to accomplish? Am I not fully aware of your potential as a person? Do you think I am not glad to direct you into a life spent in the best use of that potential?

In my company you will find your way . . . for I am the Way!

But so many are afraid to release control to me. They are afraid I may expect too much from them. How little they know of the abundant happiness I bestow on those who walk in my way!

But the Way is narrow. There is only one way whereby

149

anyone can come into the family of the Most High. Only one way one can know me as their Father and have my gracious Holy Spirit as their constant companion. That is the way of your Brother, Jesus, who surrendered His life fully to my greater Life. He showed you the Way.

A million deceptive voices—speaking with sweet reasonableness—will insist, "All paths lead to God!" This is a lie and not the truth. It is in fact the broad road, the popular path ... and it leads millions upon millions to outer darkness. You need only to visit the regions of earth where false philosophies, unbridled humanism, degrading religions, evil spirit worship, or paganism prevails—and you will soon see how people live in abject bondage, fear, and despair.

Consider
the tyranny of totalitarianism
the degradation and poverty of Hinduism
the violence and harshness of Islam
the false-god worship of paganism
the sinister nature of the occult.

These are but a small handful of the so-called *ways* to which people are attracted. Each of these *ways* have their prophets and promoters. Each insists it holds ultimate truth. Each employs subtle propaganda to persuade the gullible that it leads to God. But it is a god of their own making.

Amid all this cacophony of confusing voices ... I am the Way. I am the Truth. I am the Life. I stand amid the masses of humanity and call everyone to myself. The invitation is so simple, the response so straightforward. Most miss it.

For my way is not to make you gods in some afterlife ... or to give your soul escape into mindless bliss. My Way is the way of the spiritual child ... inwardly at rest in my care, outwardly obedient to my direction.

My way is to make you a child in spirit.

Everything in your human culture works against your coming to me like a child.

Your so-called "wise ones"—your thinkers, scholars, gurus, false prophets, religious zealots, and politicos all expound at great length on "the best way." But they are confused and in despair! Their end will be chaos, if they do not turn to me. Billions of human beings across the cruel centuries of human history have listened to the errors of men like these false leaders.

Do you hear my voice, child? I am your Father!

No one in all the earth calls you to the Way of supreme peace of spirit.

No one else gives you faith to triumph over trouble.

No one else fills you with unending joy.

No one else assures you of so much hope, both in this life and in the life to come.

Only as my spiritual child can you overcome your world.

Will you be my child? Will you seek an actual encounter between my presence and your person? I mean, quite literally, that you must bring the whole of your being into a life-changing contact with all of my being. Know me *in person*—that is, in a dynamic interaction between your spirit and mine.

I do not mean that you should simply gain more intellectual awareness of me. Millions and millions can claim to know something about a world leader. They can see his picture, listen to his broadcast voice, read his biography. Yet out of those millions of admirers only a handful of close intimates will ever really know the man! Only a small inner circle will share his mind, his emotions, his inner will of steel, his incandescent spirit.

It is the same with me. Multitudes know about me. But only a handful truly know me spirit to Spirit . . . the way a child knows its father's heart.

※

There is a special dimension you can add to life, day by day. You can discover loyalty to me, deep devotion, fervent faith, eager enthusiasm, unabashed love, and childlike delight in my company, never-ending gratitude, open and transparent pleasure in sharing my Life. These are proof positive that you know me, and I in turn know you. Proof that we are on intimate terms.

There is nothing mysterious about the beautiful relationship that can exist between us. Child, I am the Way. . . .

Live at rest in me, and I will live out my power and delightful activity through you.

Read, reflect, and in faith respond to:

John 1:1–14; 14:1–14
Matthew 7:13–14, 21–23
Ephesians 1:2–12
Proverbs 12:28; 14:12; 26:25
Romans 8:31–39

16

"I Am Righteous and Just"

*I*n all my ways ... in all my actions ... in all my attitudes ... I am Righteous and Just.

No doubt this is extremely difficult for you to understand, much less *believe.* How can your limited imagination begin to comprehend the breadth and length of my righteousness ... my justice.

I do not wonder.

⸺∞⸺

In the world of man-made laws, there is no such thing as absolute justice. Many nations have boasted about jus-

155

tice, liberty, and freedom for all—but in truth that has proven to be an illusion. For their citizens soon discover that, because of human fallibility, there can be no undeviating equality. Courts demonstrate that there is one law for the wealthy . . . and another for the poor. Societies are shot through with segregation of a hundred sorts. From their earliest years, your children are taught discrimination, taunting, and teasing one another mercilessly.

Yes, people protest for more liberty, freedom, law, and justice. But in the rub of everyday life it simply is absent. That is because the heart of man is not fair or just, not righteous in its attitudes or actions.

But I do not deviate from what is right. I am absolutely just in all I do with you. I exercise equality for everyone. I am forever fair. This is one of the most profound differences between men and me. A facet of my character that sets me apart from humanity and its corruption.

And my righteous justice is why so many hold me at arm's length. . . .

Many of your leaders have been tyrants and tormentors. You imagine I must be a monster, too. You cannot believe that I am benevolent, and not a brute.

But what strange creatures you are!

From the most ancient times, the human imagination has devised all sorts of grotesque gods. Your religions have been based upon cruel, fearsome gods. Gods who are greedy. Vengeful. Ruthless. Evil. Little wonder that masses have been deceived into offering sacrifices and repeating empty prayers, hoping their good deeds will outweigh their bad behavior.

But all the rites and all the rituals will not put you

right. For I, the true God, do not look for your sacrifices, your services, or your self-justification.

I come looking for *you.*

Good news! *Good news!* You, who have encountered so much injustice; you who have suffered so much adversity from one another; you who have endured so much wrong—I am Righteous and Just.

Come into my company. Find out firsthand that I am fair in all my dealings with you. You will be astonished at my understanding: See how freely I pardon.

I do not deal out evil for evil, malice for malice, anger for anger. My every intention toward you is couched in an attitude that is right and fair, with full understanding of your plight. Above all I deal with you as your Father, in the hope that you will let me lead you in the paths of righteousness.

If you can grasp this truth—that I am Righteous and Just in all my ways—it will change your attitude toward me. No longer will you dread me, or misconstrue my motives, or equate me with others who treat you unjustly.

You can count on me. For I am fair. Never have I been like the gods of earth. They were made by men and not by me. How is it fair of you to think I am like them?

<hr />

My power lies in justice. Not justice that binds you but divine justice that sets you free.

Free from your fear of revenge. Free from your foreboding about divine retribution. Your emancipation from fear is possible because I paid the price for all your misconduct. I set right our relationship in my generosity. I have stood in your place in the prisoner's chains: I have suffered in your stead; I have borne the brunt of your accusations; I have borne the charges against you. *I have made you go free.*

> Now you are righteous because I am Righteous.
> Now you are justified because I am Just.
> Now you are accepted because I am Fair...
> Now you are my child because I am your Father.
> Now you are my beloved because I am your Friend.

This transaction—my life for your life—makes it possible for you to be re-created in your whole character.

As you receive my righteousness and my justice, you are born into a brand-new life. It comes from me, imparted into you by my presence ... expressed through you by my Spirit, a plan that activates you. My righteous and just Life grows to full fruition in your life. This is my plan.

To know me is to share in my eternal life. To know me is to be called and made strong to go out into the world to extend justice, righteousness, and fair treatment to others. Freely you have received great gifts from me; now freely give them to those who suffer and groan. You will find your gladness and life as you enter into my service.

Down the long avenue of human history ... littered with carnage and cruelty ... my children—who are called by my name and bear my character—they have brought relief from terrible atrocities. Down to this very day in which you live, injustice, torture, violence, crime, and civil war tear your people to pieces. The earth is stained with the gore and tears of the innocent. And it is you, my child, who can comfort. It is you who can bring food, medical aid, and spiritual healing. Through you I would right wrongs!

Never listen to the lies propagated by my foes—those who claim I do not count, who ridicule and reject my followers. In times of trouble, they are the first to turn to my children for help and relief. When all is well they despise me and declare I am dead. But just let disaster befall...!

I will not hide the truth from you. Bearing my righteousness and justice to the world is costly. Even though I send you out to do great good, you are likely to be despised and rejected by men. As they rejected me, they will reject you. But my word to you is this: "Overcome evil with good." For where evil abounds, there my grace abounds even more.

Do not grow weary in your well-doing. Your confidence in me overcomes the world. Have courage, and carry on in my might.

How can you face down evil with good? I will tell you.

In making commitments—carry them out.

In making promises—fulfill them.

In taking on tasks—do them thoroughly though others shirk.

In taking on responsibilities—accomplish them though others are lazy and quit.

In taking on friends—be considerate of them.

Whatever you do: Be fair, be just, be right.

Then even my enemies will know that I am just and right, as you become a credit to my name among men.

Let righteousness and justice be your trademarks, just as they are mine.

If I live and move and have my earthly dwelling in you,

and if you live and move and have your being in me—then your character and conduct must be like mine. Do not say one thing but do another. Consistency will be your badge of honor.

Never exploit or manipulate others for your own ends. Do not take advantage of those who are weak or poor. Do not drive hard bargains in business. Do not abuse anyone or anything that is in your care. Do not always insist on being first.

These tactics may be used by the world to push ahead—but they are not the way of justice and righteousness to which I call you. If you want to live with me in harmony, goodwill, and mutual respect, you must be fair as I am forever fair with you. In your world, so motivated by self-interest, stand out as one who is fair.

To be fair is not feeble. To be fair in its fullest expression means being strong and firm for the right. Firm in your

convictions
discharge of duty
faith in me
refusal to be fickle.

If you are fair, you will be firm in goodness.

Live rightly, in justice and fairness. Call the world to me in this way. For the day of reckoning will come to all ... and you are my hands and my voice ... to warn, to inspire ... to welcome rebels home.

Read, reflect, and in faith respond to:

Deuteronomy 32:1–12
Psalms 7:9–17; 103:1–22
Revelation 16:5
I Samuel 15:10–26
Colossians 2:6–15
John 17:1–21
Hebrews 11:32–40; 12:1–13
Romans 5:20–21

17

"I Am Holy"

*Y*es, I am Holy.
     I am Perfect.
 I am Brightness ... and endless Beauty!

In my full Person I am beyond the ability of human language to describe. Yet some of my children, during the span of human history, have tried to tell others of my splendor. And it was the impulse of my own gracious self-revealing Spirit that gave them a glimpse of my glory. Because of me they cried out in words of wonder, awe, and adoration.

Because I show myself to men ... in my purity and perfection, I am called

the Altogether Lovely One
the Lily of the Valley
the Morning Star.

Each is a touching attempt to tell you even a little about my character. It follows—does it not—that those who know me best, love me best? And they have known me as ... Holy.

⸺⧟⸺

It is a sad thing that in the world the word *holy* has been distorted. Most associate it with musty church buildings, morbid music, painted haloes around the heads of plaster saints—and phoney piety that is painful for me to watch.

You find this repulsive to your souls. And so you should. For all of it is a dreadful deception, a gross delusion that has kept many of you from ever coming to know me as I truly am—*the Holy One.*

To be holy is to be
whole
complete
wholesome
healthy
perfect
pure.

To be holy is to be like me ... beautiful! But not distant, morbid, condemning, unapproachable. Quite the opposite!

⸺⧟⸺

In essence, in nature, in character ... I am *altogether*

lovely. I am lovable. You can draw near to me without mortal fear.

Do you still think of me as a despot, who stands over you in pride and power? I am your Savior! Your Shepherd! The Power of your power—Breath of your breath. Come and behold the loveliness of my behavior toward you. Taste the sweetness of my Spirit, more delectable than honey. Come in lowliness of soul, and find that in my holiness I am meek and lowly—eager to bring healing to your heart and hope to all your days!

Because I am *whole,* you can be whole.

Because I am *health,* you can be made well.

Because I am *complete,* you can become fulfilled.

Because I am *pure,* you too can be clean.

Because I am *perfect,* you can be beautiful in me.

Share in my supernatural life—and share in the beauty of my holiness. Together, we are wholesome in a rotting world.

You see, my child, I am not as fearsome and complicated as worldly scholars, theologians, and academics have made me. None of their legalisms, theories, or rituals ever made a single soul *holy.* But I re-create a new spirit in you. I form in you my own complete character. I polish you to a shine with my own beauty.

The world wants you to fear and avoid me. I want to make you perfectly lovely in holiness.

———⚬⚬⚬———

In all these quiet talks we have had together, I have tried to help you understand what I am really like. Now I invite you to receive me ... not only as your fellow companion, your fondest friend, and your holy Father—but as your Beloved!

I am not asking of you something mystical or strange. I am only asking that you accept me as I am. I have given of myself to you in terms you can understand. I have poured my heart out to you in passion. I even impart to you my faith, so you can take me at my Word . . . and trust me!

Take my life into you. Assimilate my eternal, holy nature. Be satisfied, saturated, set at rest, in wholeness and health. Be healed from the fever of your old life. Partake of me as you would break and eat bread: Drink of me as you would drink refreshment from a cup.

I have done my part in giving all of myself to you freely, without charge and without payment. If you wish to be made whole, give me all of yourself! In this exchange you will never be the same again. Just as light from the sun purifies everything exposed to its rays, all of your failings are purified as my life grows in you.

Let me tell you how I see you—how I envision the person you can be. . . .

You will become a truly beautiful individual. For my beauty shall be yours.

You will be winsome, wonderfully wholesome. For I make you whole.

You will not be a stiff, staid, stilted "saint"—in the false guise of somber godliness.

Rather, you will brim over with irrepressible life and delight. Peace and well-being is the portion of those who know me in person. Power, purity, and perfection will prove my presence in you. In your daily walk with me, you will actually become a holy individual—and at the same time, you yourself will remain humbly aware that the superb wholeness is not your own. For I love to reside with anyone who is humble in heart.

No, your world cannot understand these things. They cannot perceive the power or purity of my presence. But you can

know me
love me
honor me
enjoy me
trust me
follow me
obey me.

My beloved child, before the foundation of the earth I had set my love upon you. Before time I ordained that there would be sons and daughters whom I would adopt as my holy children. They would be my chosen—made complete in my company.

And from the beginning I knew that one of them would be you!

———

And now I set the special seal of my own Holy Spirit upon you. You are my prized possession. You have been made my child, in a plan that has unfolded with deliberate care from eternity. My perfect life, perfect death, and perfect power paid for *you*.

The insights I have shared with you are given to breathe life into your soul. I tell you now: Beyond your brief life on earth, I have prepared for you a marvelous home. And there you will reside with me forever. There is no sorrow there—no sadness, no suffering, no sin, no Satan. And only the holy, the undefiled, enter there!

That is why I go to such pains to prepare *you* for that

place. Do not be dismayed, for I am the Author of your wholeness—and the Finisher of your holiness.

All that you are or ever will be has its beginning and its end in me. I claim you as my own, forever and forever.

This is the Word I leave you: "Know me—for to know me is Life eternal!"

Read, reflect, and in faith respond to:

Isaiah 6:1–8
Song of Solomon 2:1–4
Matthew 11:25–30
John 1:12; 14:9–23; 15:1–16
Psalm 37:1–40
1 Corinthians 2:1–16

A Note of Thanks

All through this work there has been an acute awareness of our Father's presence. The close companionship of Christ and clear guidance of His gracious Spirit have been the inspiration in the writing: a distinct honor! In awe and humility, genuine praise and gratitude are poured out from my whole being.

Again, hearty, hearty thanks are given to Fern Webber, not only for her professional expertise in the word processing but also for her joyous goodwill. Such a blessing!

There are dear friends, some nearby, others scattered across the earth, who have prayed earnestly for this endeavor. Thank you, thank you, for your kind faithfulness!

Last, but most heartily, my gratitude is extended to Ursula for her encouragement and fortitude.